Moritz Rinke

THE MAN WHO NEVER YET SAW
WOMAN'S NAKEDNESS

(*Der Mann, Der Noch Keiner Frau Blösse Entdeckte*)

Translated by Meredith Oakes

~

Katharina Gericke

WARWESER

(*Maienschlager*)

Translated by David Tushingham

T0262495

OBERON BOOKS
LONDON

Maienschlager first published by Henschel SCHAUSPIEL Theaterverlag, Berlin GmbH in 1995

First published in this collection in 2001 by Oberon Books Ltd.
(incorporating Absolute Classics)
521 Caledonian Road, London N7 9RH
Tel: 020 7607 3637 / Fax: 020 7607 3629
e-mail: oberon.books@btinternet.com

A catalogue record for this book is available from the British Library.

ISBN: 978-1-8400-2229-2

Cover illustration: Andrzej Klimowski
Cover typography: Jeff Willis

Contents

Preface

In November 1999 the Royal Court Theatre in London hosted a German Playreading Season, its fourth since 1993, organised in association with the Goethe-Institut London. The season featured five plays by new playwrights from Germany in specially commissioned English translations. A few months later, two of these plays – *Mr Kolpert* by David Gieselmann and *Fireface* by Marius von Mayenburg – were presented in fully fledged productions as part of the Royal Court's International Playwrights season 2000. Another play, *King Kong's Daughters* by Theresia Walser, is included in the Theatre Library of the Goethe-Institut, a collection of contemporary German-language plays to which four new works are added each year. I am delighted that the two remaining plays – *Warweser* by Katharina Gericke and *The Man Who Never Yet Saw Woman's Nakedness* by Moritz Rinke – have now also been made available in print.

Katharina Gericke and Moritz Rinke are very exciting new voices in German drama. Their plays have been performed to great acclaim throughout Germany, and they have both received important awards. Meredith Oakes and David Tushingham have produced excellent translations of their plays, *Warweser* and *The Man Who Never Yet Saw Woman's Nakedness*, and I hope that this volume may inspire theatre directors in English-speaking countries to put them on stage.

Barbara Honrath
Head of Arts,
Goethe-Institut
London, 2001

n of *The Man Who Never Yet Saw Woman's*
first performed as a rehearsed reading on 12
9 at The Royal Court Theatre, London, with
ast:

nily Bruni
CHT, Chiwetel Ejiofor
E STONE, Roger Evans
n Foley

oxana Silbert
, Andreas Beck
er, Jayne Aplin

THE MAN WHO NEVER YET SAW WOMAN'S NAKEDNESS

(Der Mann, Der Noch Keiner Frau Blösse Entdeckte)

'And woe to the stranger
Who travels out of love
And comes upon such a people...'
Hölderlin
(Hyperion to Bellarmin)

This translati
Nakedness was
November 19
the following

ANNA, E
HELMBR
PETER/TI
FELIX, S

Director, I
Play Advis
Stage Mana

THE FIRST DAY

1. Waiting for the play

Evening. An empty room. A wall at the back. Chairs in front of it.
Darkness. Time passes. And now: someone runs through the room.
Falls. Runs on, to the wall at the side. Light. A young man is holding
six mugs in his hands. Eight cups hang from his fingers, and four
exotic blooms are balanced between his teeth, while in his arms are
two balldresses, thirty-five chocolate bars and a sword. He runs to
the middle. Turns. A pause. He turns back.

YOUNG MAN: I'm here… (*He turns, calls.*) Hullo! (*He turns
back.*) I mean, I… (*Not a word can be understood. He drops
the exotic blooms from his mouth on to the floor.*) So. All this
is my responsibility. (*Pause.*) I always bring all this. That
I can do. It's part of my work. It means I can set the
mood instantly. (*He runs to the left. Looks.*) I'm talking
about portable feelings. (*He runs to the right. Looks.*) A
bloom like this for each of them straight away. Then
coffee. Aiming of kisses. And a professional declaration
of love. (*In the pose of a professional declaration of love.*)
Your expression! Your bearing! The way you speak!
(*Falls to his knees.*) What a presence! (*Breaks off.*) Like
Rudolf Valentino. They all love me. (*He turns. Pause. He
turns back.*) The balcony scene is no picnic. He said: The
balcony scene is a purely human moment. It isn't enough
just to signal it. It needs months – and that's all it needs
– sinking into the consciousness of the team. (*He puts the
mugs and cups on a chair and throws the rest on to the floor.*)
A bomb scare. Could be. It could be a Palestinian date
bomb. It happens. (*He drinks coffee.*) Installed in a 'lotus
plum' date. Smuggled into a public place. There's a brief
detonation, triggered by the chewing action of the
incisors. Around two hundred and fifty victims
worldwide. In theory. (*Drinks.*) There are people standing
around somewhere in the world as we speak, not
thinking about anything in particular, suddenly someone
feels like a 'lotus plum'. (*Drinks.*) Evil can no longer be

detected by the naked eye. I mean: last month I made a speech. (*Drinks.*) In a plane. (*Drinks.*) I made a speech, because the air hostess gave the man in front of me a Lebanese diarrhoea pill. God! A Lebanese diarrhoea pill is just mass murder. I was two hours convincing economy class that on technical and health grounds it was better for all of us if he did without his Lebanese diarrhoea pill. (*He jumps up.*) Am I doing everything on my own here? (*Pause.*) Hullo? (*He takes the exotic blooms and silently practises the professional declaration of love.*) Rudolf Valentino! (*He runs to the telephone. Dials a number.*) I'm not drinking seven litres of coffee on my own. It's supposed to be the balcony scene. We need a purely human... Hullo? (*He hangs up. Runs to the centre. Sits between the ballgowns. Long pause.*) Right. It's all a disaster. Nevertheless, it's my department. Bad news. Good news. It's often the way. Good. Bad. Bad. Good. I'm no philosopher. Although it would be interesting to know if one of them came first... (*He turns.*) – Angela? (*Pause. He turns back. He takes the plants. Kneeling, he practises the professional declaration of love.*) I'm asking you. Is it the case, that one comes into the world thinking: wonderful. Thank you. This is a really good start – and then later says: You bastard. Even I could do better... Or is it the other way around: I immediately recognise the full extent of the mortal elements in life – bombs in lotus plums, Lebanese diarrhoea pills and so on – but then later I think: No, but you and your friends would have all been looking fantastically old, if one hadn't... (*Breaks off the professional declaration of love.*) Bad. Good. Good. Bad. I sometimes think for instance – Think of Christ on the cross. Good. It's maybe all a bit hasty writing the whole world off, if you just reflect that I did actually come and... Well. Words. Words, and the person who understands them and who ultimately recognises them as meaningless, when he's got through them – and above them – and out over the top of them: Sorry! So he's hanging there on the cross, from the dreadful nails, looks down and sees John running around frantically. He calls out, 'John, quick, come here.' 'I'm coming,' shouts

John, and climbs up the cross pelted with stones by Christ's tormentors and reaches the top covered in blood. And Jesus? Jesus says: 'Look, John. I can see your house from here.'
(*The light goes out.*)
Ah. (*Pause.*) It seems very dark suddenly. (*Pause.*) I may have turned into a cup of coffee. It happens. (*He runs in the dark.*) When he awoke one morning... (*Falls.*) from troubled dreams, he found himself transformed in his bed... (*Runs.*) – into a monstrous cup of coffee. (*Pause.*) Peter? (*Pause.*) He was lying on his caffeinated back and could see...
(*Suddenly light again.*)
...by lifting his...totally...caffeinated...head...

2. In the Promised Land

Front, in a chair: A young man. Wrapped in wet linen – barefoot and dazzled by the light. He is holding a big rock of amber, and wearing a helmet. He's very cold.

FELIX: And who are you?
(*The YOUNG MAN IN LINEN jumps up, startled. They stare at each other without moving.*)
Hullo.
(*Silence.*)
Are you the new man?
(*Silence.*)
Are you? – aha – hullo?
(*Silence.*)
Hm. (*Pause.*) What's the weather like, still bad?
(*Silence.*)
Yes. (*Pause.*) Interesting headgear!
(*Silence.*)
Jesus on the cross looks down and sees John. Stop me if you've heard it. (*Pause.*) I know others.
(*Silence.*)
Right. (*Pause.*) Now I understand. (*As if to a foreigner.*)
You're a visitor. Welcome!
(*Silence. He waves.*)

Hullo? You have to play a ball to me sometimes. Is that stone heavy? (*Pause.*) You're not saying – hm. (*Pause.*) Well, I'm Felix.

FELIX: And who are you?

(*Silence.*)

This can't be happening. Who actually said you could... hey!

(*Silence.*)

We're in a play about a man and a fish. (*Pause.*) Do you like fish? (*Pause.*) Because – I mean – they don't talk much either. Hullo!

(*Silence.*)

FELIX: It's great being with you!

(*He throws his cup of coffee at the wall. The YOUNG MAN IN LINEN drops the stone. He shrinks back. Listens. Stands still. His gaze looks like that of a child waking up. He moves his lips. Brings one foot forward. Hesitantly half lifts an arm, on whose hand the fingers rise and fall in front of the torso – as if feeling for a space on behalf of the rest of the body. A place. A counterpart. Or a memory. He begins to speak, softly and then more audibly.*)

YOUNG MAN IN LINEN: Storms – fire – ice – snow – swords. Fearful to behold, the weather. Heaven cried out – Death fell in the rain of ash the eagle... (*He turns.*) – flapped, flag of the mighty host invading – blood hail rained need loss and cold... (*Turns back.*) – years – wandering – exile... (*Holds one hand to his temple, as if trying to ease an inner chaos or fury.*) – Then His great flight, fleeing twice three thousand furlongs, more... (*Staggers, looking about.*) – the false west wind behind him – (*Staggers.*) – a fading scream behind him – a thought... (*Sinks down on his stone.*) If only that day were clay. Thick the darkness, no light. Not given to him to see behind him.

(*Silence. Then, as if against his will, driven by the words, he begins again.*)

YOUNG MAN IN LINEN: Storms – fire – ice – snow – swords. Fearful to behold, the weather. Heaven cried –

FELIX: ...Stop!

YOUNG MAN IN LINEN: ...out...

FELIX: Thank you. Yes. We read yesterday. You should make an appointment, you shouldn't just appear in the middle of our work process, which is so important, in this overdramatic way. It's the evening rehearsal! Besides, we're based entirely in the present. Your monologue. No-one's going to understand it. 'Fearful to behold, the weather!?' What are you...? It sounds like... I don't know. It's not on. We don't do that now. (*Silence.*)

FELIX: Hullo? (*Pause.*) I'm sorry. I'm... You see. I'm responsible for all this. (*He turns away. Pause. He turns back.*) Would you like a coffee?

(*Gives him a cup of coffee.*

The YOUNG MAN IN LINEN stares into the cup. Then he does as FELIX does. Both drink.)

This is good coffee. I've perfected it. I know all about these things. Look: these blooms. Have you any idea how much stress I can avoid with these. See this: Why do I always bring along this chocolate? Yes. It's peace offerings. Blocks of it. Edelbitter. At least till they start complaining about the costumes. Then there's nothing to be done. You know: they eat so much when they're working. Sometimes I work with roast chicken. Think of it. Ten in the morning, roast chicken, then Euripides, *Iphigenia in Aulis.* On one hand, ancient wellsprings of drama. On the other, modern smell of chips. The result was horrendous. But my communications technique, brilliant. (*Drinks.*) I studied engineering science for a term. My mother always thought I should learn how to care for the sick. But my father argued all his life in favour of engineering science. There was one brief interlude, when with this huge razor he used to have he severed an artery in his neck. My mother got the upper hand at that point. He decided for a while I should study trauma surgery, but then it was back to engineering science. Listen son: steel and concrete construction. Mining. Smelting systems. That's real. Go ahead and read your Mao and your Rudi Dutschke. Fall asleep in your feather bed over your communist books, we've all done that. But think about it: engineering science!

(*Drinks.*) Heavens, you're all wet. Why are you wet? I'll get you the hair dryer. You need the hair dryer.

(*FELIX off. He comes back, an extension cord trailing behind him. The YOUNG MAN IN LINEN stands motionless, in one hand his cup of coffee, in the other, now, the hair dryer.*) I said: fine. I'll make bombs. Bombs are science. Do you know that bomb theory can be used to explain everything. Inside a bomb, two complete opposites are able to coexist under special circumstances for a certain amount of time. Then: only when new circumstances enter: bang! Then comes the explosion. What's more, a bomb functions exactly the same as Anna or Angela. That's what I'm saying. A fundamental theory of the world. It's a difficult subject. If you want it to dry you'll have to switch it on. God. If only I could introduce something like a new circumstance into women. They resist. They want... It's always supposed to be something fantastically strong, when weak is what you're being. And if you're strong and proud, then naturally that's supposed to be totally weak, so they can trample around with their ego well plumed, which of course I... Weak. Strong. Strong. Weak. It's a principle in women, that a delicate body can often house the soul of an iceberg, whereas one who's built like a filing cabinet can be harbouring tropical passions. According to Schopenhauer. No. I'm Schopenhauer. I'm simply trying to counter their partner concept. I think I just want a natural female surrender. An outburst of feeling finally resolved in the other's masculinity. A quite primitive man-woman ecstasy. A human moment, you can't just...

(*The hairdryer starts. The YOUNG MAN IN LINEN dries himself. First, hesitantly and doubtfully, his hands, then more bravely his neck, then blissfully hair and helmet. Then, full of the joy of discovery, he switches off.*)

YOUNG MAN IN LINEN: Brothers came. Brothers fought and found death. The stars fell from the sky. We carried dreams through poisoned valleys. That was the sword time. Storm time. Wolf time. And then: he wished to fight no more. He was tired. (*He takes off his helmet. Switches on again. Dries. Is about to speak. Switches off.*) He asked: Down with Rome? – and you stay and fall into the earth. Out of the country? – and you simply go abroad. (*He climbs onto a chair.*) The meadow lies before him. There is a world beyond his hut. Forward. Onward. Fly. Better. Freer. Coffee!

(*Silence.*)

FELIX: Coffee? – Of course, coffee. More coffee.

(*Both drink.*)

Good. I like you. I used to be just the same as you. The conviction. The shining goal along the dark road from which no step was to deviate. What are you actually called?

(*Silence.*)

Say a name to me, you astonishing talent.

(*The YOUNG MAN IN LINEN begins gently to move his head about as if searching for a different rhythm. Then, at first astonished and cautious, soon with the confidence of long-pent-up curiosity – as if someone were seeing themselves for the first time in a mirror – falteringly he murmurs the name.*)

YOUNG MAN IN LINEN: Helmbrecht.

(*Silence.*)

FELIX: Helmbrecht! (*Pause.*) That's a very unusual name. (*Big gesture.*) Whoever you are, I want to help you!

(*HELMBRECHT gets down from the stool. He slowly runs towards FELIX. Stops. Hesitates. Moves his head about again. There is now a slight smile on his face. He stretches out his hand to FELIX.*)

HELMBRECHT: Joy to mankind – the gods rage no longer. (*He rests his forehead on FELIX's chest.*) The god has made you great-hearted. (*Pause.*) Have you food?

(*Silence.*)

FELIX: You should give some consideration to your grammar. It should be more flowing: looser. 'Joy to mankind' – It just doesn't sound loose. It won't get you… Look: we should never use a noun, where we can use a verb. Go on with your speech.

(*Silence.*)

Hullo! Go on! (*Pause.*) Or I'll christen you Gottlieb Klopstock!

(*HELMBRECHT climbs on to the chair.*)

HELMBRECHT: The young man who never yet saw woman's nakedness, have you seen him?

FELIX: What?

HELMBRECHT: Yes, they gave him a stone, but he's so alone with the stone.

FELIX: Yes but keep to the subject.

HELMBRECHT: Dear gods – (*He weeps.*)

FELIX: Gods. Stone. Woman's nakedness...

HELMBRECHT: ...Shall a lion rise up to dwarf the race of men? Shall a power come, bringing beauty? The God they speak of, he wants to see him! Then: Reach with your eyes to the ends of the earth. Just hold the earth still. And take off your shoes: Now he gets down. (*He gets down from the chair.*)

FELIX: The grammar's improving. But the content?! (*He turns away. He turns back.*) That's enough games. What do you want?

HELMBRECHT: Red...blue...and green. Yellow green, perfumed. And gold. And real laughter. Under a new sky – pink and blue. No black flag of the brothers. Blooms like that! Communication chocolate! It has to glitter. We have to live. Be dazzled. See nothing more. Never again. But knowing: It was. More coffee please.
(*Silence.*)

FELIX: Are you going to do this the whole time? (*Pause.*) I won't be able to stand it. What is it you're spouting? (*Silence.*)
(*HELMBRECHT again begins moving his head about gently, as if experimenting with different rhythms. Then – his head lowered as if in childlike shame – falteringly he now murmurs the word.*)

HELMBRECHT: Helogermanic.
(*Silence.*)
Helogermanic is father and mother's language. It's spoken in deep mutual reverence.

FELIX: Right. What about the rest of the time? What do you speak the rest of the time?
(*As HELMBRECHT moves his head to and fro, he holds one hand, then the other, flat in front of his temples, as if seeking a decision, a resolution, between left and right.*)

HELMBRECHT: Melogermanic. Melogermanic is what Helmbrecht is speaking at the moment. (*Pause.*) 'Fearful to behold, the weather – (*Pause.*) – is Helogermanic. 'The young man who never yet saw woman's nakedness – did you see him?' – (*Pause.*) Helogermanic and Melogermanic together. Helogermanic is – (*Pause.*) – right of the Rhine. (*Pause.*) We vanish in the face of the gods – (*Pause.*) – behind language. Melogermanic – (*Pause.*) – is different. Left of the Rhine. With Melogermanic we're speaking as – (*Pause.*) – the gods. Helogermanic! (*He attempts to stop the seeking movements, and hits the back of his head with his hand.*) Helogermanic is only spoken now in the huts of the fathers. Outside, in front of the Romans, you have to speak Melogermanic. The Romans all speak Melogermanic.

FELIX: I beg your pardon?

HELMBRECHT: The Romans all speak Melogermanic.

FELIX: Yes. So you know some Romans, and you speak with them?

HELMBRECHT: Yes that's right. They call themselves brothers and they travelled to the edge of the world. It's right of the Rhine under the black sky. You feel a foreboding when the black sky is spoken about. First they opened markets and gave us coins and the friends were as if changed overnight. The world was a different place and even the sky looked gentler and milder. Do you like bison?

FELIX: What? Yes... Oh yes.

HELMBRECHT: You feel a longing when oxen are spoken about. Helmbrecht honours bison and cared for them all his life – until the brothers came with a smile. Once there was the justice of the gods and the blade of the ploughshare if a man stole another man's holy things. But then, when the smiling came and the friends learned there were laws crueller than the laws of weapons, the blades rusted. What remained was the shock, when your eye fell from the smiling down to the sly hands. Oh, they should call the deep Rhine, who hid his pain, to rise and give his answer to the world. (*Pause.*) Felix?

FELIX: Yes.

HELMBRECHT: What's a feather bed?

(*Silence.*)

FELIX: Do you think we've all just been waiting for you to come along?

(*Silence.*)

FELIX: A feather bed? – Yes...you – it's something very... important. Our fathers have always lain with our mothers on feather beds, and thought about a thing... (*He turns around.*) – that's always been a fundamental decision, even though anyone can... (*He turns back.*) – How did you get in?

(*Silence.*)

HELMBRECHT: Father lay with mother in the barn. They left him sleeping, when they went. The friends who found them with the stone – (*Pause.*) – under the water, because they couldn't pay the tax any more – had carried them back into the barn again – (*His hand presses on his temple as if it's having to hold his head together.*) His mother's eyes looked so far into the distance – He looked into them – Nothing in him remained in place. That was at an end forever. Everything in him went there. To where no-one knows what happens. (*He sinks down on his stone. Silence.*) His mother had buttered bread for him at sunrise. When he awoke, she was gone. Only the bread and butter were there. A whole table full. And a tree with one leaf and her words: When the tree is grown tall in our woods, then you will wait no more. He never saw her again.

(*Silence. FELIX runs to the telephone. He dials a number.*)

FELIX: If I could just get through in this place... Hullo? – Unbelievable!

HELMBRECHT: Guess how many bison he used to have.

FELIX: Heavens, a hundred!

HELMBRECHT: Yes! That's right. He had two hundred before, but he had to give a hundred because of Dietlinde. Dietlinde is the wife of Heilmar. He who covets his friend's wife must give bison. Fifteen for stroking her hand, thirty-five for the top of the arm. Breast touching is fifty. Ah, when you long for happiness so much. You have to take it in your hands for once and hold it tight in your arms and drink it down.

FELIX: Oh Helmbrecht, both breasts!

HELMBRECHT: Yes, that's right.

FELIX: Yes, that's right! Are you a plate short of a picnic? Coming in here as cool as... Why do you lug that rock around?

HELMBRECHT: We always do that. You should listen to stones. They're older. They know more. They contain a lot of time. It's not cramped in stones. (*Pause*). Felix?

FELIX: Yes!

HELMBRECHT: Is it winter? (*Pause.*) If it's winter, it's important to greet the first snowflakes. You can be amazed. You can love the silence. (*Pause.*) Felix?

FELIX: Yes.

HELMBRECHT: We should embrace a sunset. Let's embrace a sunset.

FELIX: Listen, we'll have to wait for a while.

HELMBRECHT: What are we waiting for?

FELIX: For the sun to set!

HELMBRECHT: But isn't it always setting? Wasn't it always setting, before? (*Pause.*) Felix?

FELIX: Helmbrecht.

HELMBRECHT: He used to have a dog.

FELIX: Aha.

HELMBRECHT: Then it died.

FELIX: Hm.

HELMBRECHT: They took the dog out of his arms and ate it. There was nothing else. Now he's got the stone instead of the dog. (*Pause.*) Felix?

FELIX: Last question, all right?

HELMBRECHT: What are smelting systems?

FELIX: Smelting systems?

HELMBRECHT: You said smelting systems.

FELIX: You're right, I did. Yes, they're systems for smelting things.

HELMBRECHT: What things can you smelt?

FELIX: Everything. Crystalline. Amorphous. That helmet. That stone. Bison. Romans too. I can smelt everything into everything else. Even you!

(*He goes off, with the hairdryer. HELMBRECHT stands there motionless. Long pause.*)

HELMBRECHT: Oh. He could put in some of the communications chocolate. Some gold and laughter – Dietlinde. Snowflakes. And the sunsets.

(*Long pause. HELMBRECHT stares upwards. He shuts his eyes and stands there. Long pause. He opens his eyes. Takes a step to the side. Then: He embraces the air in the spot where he has just been standing with his eyes closed. Long pause. FELIX returns.*)

FELIX: We have to reach an understanding here. This can't continue. How can… I mean… What are you doing?

(*HELMBRECHT continues to embrace the air.*)

Hullo?

(*HELMBRECHT embraces the air.*)

I'm sorry. Could you stop that – Hey! (*Pause.*) That's enough!

HELMBRECHT: It's gone! (*Pause.*) Oh. That was a beautiful embrace. (*Pause.*) We always do that. You think about something as hard as you can. Then step aside. Then, embrace your thought.

(*Silence. FELIX off without comment.*
HELMBRECHT rushes over to the ballgown.
FELIX returns.)

FELIX: Helmbrecht, yes? Just Helmbrecht, Helmbrecht the Hun, yes?

HELMBRECHT: Yes, that's right.

(*FELIX off.*
HELMBRECHT looks at the ballgown.
FELIX returns.)

FELIX: And you just couldn't stand the Romans any more so you came all the way here?

HELMBRECHT: Yes, that's…

FELIX: OK.

FELIX off. HELMBRECHT compares the ballgown with the linen. FELIX returns.

FELIX: By the way. Helmbrecht: About women: You should alter your basic concept. Do you know what works? It needs a casual hat on, always look busy and never lose your reserve.

(*FELIX off.*
HELMBRECHT accidentally tears the ballgown down the middle.
FELIX returns.)
And. (*Pause.*) I've decided. (*He goes off. Dark.*)

3. Joy, divine spark

HELMBRECHT is sitting on the floor. He's carefully trying to fit the two pieces of the ballgown together. Then HELMBRECHT looks to the heavens. He dreams. FELIX returns. He's pushing trees with mandarins on them in from the left. FELIX off. HELMBRECHT runs to the mandarin trees. FELIX comes on from the right, pushing a cocktail bar, a refrigerator and music centre. FELIX presses a button on the music centre. There's Wagner or waltzes – the main thing is that it should be very attention-grabbing. FELIX off. HELMBRECHT runs towards the bar, the cocktails and the music. FELIX appears from the left pushing a bubbling fountain. FELIX off. HELMBRECHT runs towards the bubbling fountain. FELIX comes in from the right and throws down a feather mattress. FELIX off. HELMBRECHT runs backwards in the direction of the feather mattress. FELIX appears from the left pushing a bright spotlight which points at HELMBRECHT. FELIX off. HELMBRECHT holds his hands over his eyes. FELIX comes in from the right and throws a bundle of clothes into HELMBRECHT's arms. FELIX remains. Music stops.

FELIX: Start! Put those on!
    (*HELMBRECHT puts them on.*
    FELIX sits at the bar. He smokes a cigarette. HELMBRECHT is now dressed in a shirt. Well-fitting trousers. And shoes. All just like FELIX.
    FELIX gets up from the bar. He runs slowly, in an apparently ceremonial or official way, towards HELMBRECHT. He takes a cigarette out of his pocket. Puts it in HELMBRECHT's mouth. Lights it. Pause. FELIX takes a remote control out of his pocket. And now: music. And, most important: very infectious. FELIX starts dancing. He gently tugs at HELMBRECHT's arms. He pulls harder on HELMBRECHT's arms. He starts guiding HELMBRECHT's legs with his feet. HELMBRECHT is obliged to dance. He is pulled. He is pushed. He is turned.

And he begins to get into the rhythm. And now FELIX and
HELMBRECHT are a dancing pair of drunken men. Then
from the left a YOUNG WOMAN runs in.
Music stops.)

4. First exercise/Learning by Doing 1

The YOUNG WOMAN is out of breath. She's holding her shoes in
her hands. FELIX and HELMBRECHT stand motionless.

YOUNG WOMAN: Can you hear my heart? I ran and ran!
I thought: I'll never make it. How can this be
happening? Have you seen the others? It's crazy! From
one day to the next it's... My feet. Is that coffee? I saw it
in a film. It just can't be! I just took my shoes in my
hand and then...they've all gone mad. I have to have
something to drink. Didn't we both see that film? I
thought... Where are the glasses? – And you? Listening
to music, it seems very original somehow! I'll drink it as
it is. (*She drinks.*)

HELMBRECHT: (*Staring at the woman – softly.*) Aren't you
going to tie it up?

FELIX: (*Also staring at the woman.*) Tie it up? That's a funny
idea!

HELMBRECHT: If you don't tie it up, it will run off again.

FELIX: Where would it run to?

HELMBRECHT: Who knows. Anywhere. Straight on.

YOUNG WOMAN: (*Puts the bottle down.*) It was that film
with the man who lives four hundred years. And fights.
Don't you have any mineral water? And they had all
those scenes with everything collapsing. I feel dreadful.
With Angela. There were three of us at the film. That
funny night. Her. Me. You. You'd made a date with us
both without thinking.

HELMBRECHT: We need a hat. Have you got a hat?

FELIX: I don't have a hat.

YOUNG WOMAN: Heavens! Why a hat? It was a really
weird film. There must be at least five thousand dead.
Explosions! Earthquakes! Murders! You can't just pretend
it's not happening.

HELMBRECHT: If we could just introduce a new circumstance into you.

FELIX: He means it theoretically.

HELMBRECHT: It's a principle in women.

FELIX: Schopenhauer says.

YOUNG WOMAN: Schopenhauer? What about Schopenhauer? What am I talking about? What are you doing?

HELMBRECHT: We just want a natural female surrender. An outburst of feeling finally resolved in the other's masculinity. A primitive man-woman ecstasy. A sort of human moment...

FELIX: ...He who covets his friend's wife must give bison. Fifteen for stroking her hand. Thirty-five for the top of the arm. Breast touching is fifty. So!

YOUNG WOMAN: Excuse me. Have you looked out of the window?

HELMBRECHT: He's a plate short of a picnic.

FELIX: Very funny!

HELMBRECHT: Listen: Jesus is hanging on the cross, looks down and sees John. Do you know it?

YOUNG WOMAN: Felix?

FELIX: Anna.

ANNA: Who is this?

FELIX: Helmbrecht.
(*Silence.*)

HELMBRECHT: Hullo.

ANNA: Hullo.
(*Silence.*)

HELMBRECHT: If you've heard it, I could tell you a different one.
(*Silence.*)
Hullo.

ANNA: Hullo, Felix, I...

HELMBRECHT: I'll get you the hairdryer. You need the hairdryer.

FELIX: (*Fairly loud.*) For God's sake! Will you just shut up!
(*Silence. HELMBRECHT runs to his stone.*)

ANNA: You're very aggressive.

FELIX: I'm not aggressive!

ANNA: Yes you are. You're aggressive.

FELIX: All right. I'm aggressive.

ANNA: See.

FELIX: See! It's midnight. I've been waiting here for hours! No-one came! My blooms are wilting! I've drunk seven litres of coffee out of sheer desperation! And all you can say is, 'See!'

ANNA: You should be glad anyone's turned up at all.

FELIX: Yes, but it's him: he wasn't called! He just appeared out of nowhere! Meet Gottlieb Klopstock!

ANNA: What do you expect? People are running about in all directions. Why Klopstock? Somehow I find it quite clear.

FELIX: Yes, it's all absolutely clear! Now listen. I have to rehearse the balcony scene. There are three days to the revival. I'm under a certain amount of inner pressure, and what am I doing? I'm conversing with a madman out of nowhere! He knows Romans. Legions of Romans. Well you've always liked Italians. Where's Romeo?

ANNA: I keep trying to tell you. God, don't you know what...

FELIX: ...Shit. It's typical. Juliet's your role. It's a play. You don't have to try it at home. I can't bear it. Did you sleep with him?

ANNA: Sleep with him? Look, are you mad? There is no Romeo. There's no any of us. This is the end. There's nowhere left to run. Let's just stop.
(*Dark.*)

THE SECOND DAY

5. When a person takes the plunge

Morning. ANNA is sitting at the bar. HELMBRECHT, off to the side on his stone, is staring into the bubbling fountain. FELIX is standing behind, with hat, looking at the wall.

FELIX: Anna. Revolutions don't look like this. Have you ever seen a real revolution? Do you actually know my theory of revolutions? Hope as a construction of a point B, when A has become unbearable? – Yes – and then in the end, you wind up at C: and then you're disappointed. It's that simple.
(Both drink.)
ANNA: What's this.
FELIX: French Connection.
ANNA: With Southern Comfort?
FELIX: No. Amaretto. It's a Manhattan Dry with Southern Comfort.
ANNA: Without ice?
FELIX: We've run out of ice.
(Silence.)
ANNA: What are we doing now? We've sat here waiting since yesterday. We can't drink cocktails all the time. I want breakfast. I'm tired. I'd like…Felix. I wish I were somewhere else. The beauty we keep talking about, where is it? Is it simply an idea? We need to put some clothes on it and hat and shoes, so it can get out finally. Yes, why are we doing all this?
(Silence.)
FELIX: You know that erotic feeling when you're stuck in a lift together?
(Silence.)
ANNA: I think a scene like that would need you to build it up a bit more, compositionally. You're always so flat in that way.
FELIX: Really? So how about Peter? Obviously since yesterday he's been lying around in Goethestrasse,

congratulating himself on how the whole thing has
solved the balcony scene.

ANNA: Of course. Everything's always totally logical with
you.

FELIX: I'm not stupid.

ANNA: Yes you are.

FELIX: So how am I suddenly stupid? It's normal to be
jealous of Romeo, don't you think?

ANNA: I came here because of you. There are things that
are more important.

(*HELMBRECHT runs upstage. He listens with his ear to
the wall.*)

FELIX: That interests me.

ANNA: Really. Then perhaps you'd like to cast your
interest back to last Friday.

FELIX: It wasn't my fault.

ANNA: My parents were completely shocked. They wanted
to get to know you. My mother cooked cordon bleu. I
recited your entire artistic CV to my father in advance.
And you.

FELIX: Me? You spent four days coaching me to grapple
with your parents. 'Don't talk too much!' – 'Even if you
don't say "Sie", just don't say "du".' 'Make sure you
know what the Dow Jones index is, my father likes that!'
I was so tense I couldn't even hold my cup.

(*HELMBRECHT runs to another part of the back wall. He
listens.*)

ANNA: But in three hours you might at least have said
something! You didn't show any interest.

FELIX: I was instructed not to. They didn't show any
interest either. They probably knew it all anyway.

ANNA: Yes, your artistic CV. They'll think I'm going
around with a fish.

FELIX: Excuse me! In the whole evening they asked me
just two questions. Your mother: 'How old is your ex-
girlfriend?' Your father: 'And what connects the
telephone to the computer?' Marvellous! My ex-
girlfriend is twenty-seven, and the telephone is connected
to the computer by a modem. My God, what's wrong
with them.

(*HELMBRECHT runs backwards in the room, his eyes fixed on the wall.*)

ANNA: You're not generally so literal-minded. That's how it is in modern families. You start with concrete questions. What were they supposed to ask you? Whether you think democracy's a good form of government?

(*Thunder like a bomb going off in the distance. HELMBRECHT runs to his stone.*)

FELIX: The minute your father came down the stairs. That gunshot look: 'So. He's slept with my daughter!' – and then immediately to his duties. I swore to myself: I'm going to behave like an asexual lump of rock.

ANNA: Thank you! It was a really nice evening!

FELIX: You can talk! You should have seen yourself. Outwardly I was a lump of rock, but inwardly I was boiling. It was actually impossible to exchange a single sensible word with your parents because you did nothing but talk the whole time! All we could do was pay attention to you! I offer simply as an example your dessert demand. The dessert demand was really a typical scene. I know if one wants more dessert, one simply has to ask if there's more dessert. But you raised your voice, you demanded dessert from your father and acted the whole time as if your father didn't love you any more, just because he too wanted more dessert.

(*Loud thunder.*)

The worst thing was the cordon bleu incident. So you didn't like your last mouthful of cordon bleu. But was that any reason to scream and spit it on your mother's plate?

(*Louder thunder. HELMBRECHT jumps up from his stone and runs up and down.*)

HELMBRECHT: Let me advise *ma cherie* – He could spit from the very first day – The upswing has begun – And when a person takes the plunge – *Bitte am Apparat bleiben* – The only answer was the wind in the trees – Helpless as an ox before the mountain – Delay in the adjustment of tax relief – You must change your life – And what's cheaper by the dozen – Give me a basket – seven crates

of beer and eight bottles of wine, that's what I suggest –
God is far from well – We shall rock the child – If A
then B – And you start with concrete questions – *Ich
schwimme gern* – Or: I also brake for animals – Peace in
Europe – And with this I'd like to apply for – Spring is
bound to come – And strengthen my right wing – The
walls stand speechless and so cold – They are not all free
who mock their chains – Swam across: Everything's
getting better – Not the foggiest – I shall walk into the
sunset – And who will weep – If appetite grows by what
it feeds on – Or: Should a blonde come into the
supermarket – And how do the Prussians shoot – It's the
highest railway – Did you miss the bus? – Now to the
point – Whoever you are, I'll help you – And think of
happiness in a cross-section of the population – As one
looks around this noble circle – Sit with us in the first
row – Question: plop hiss bubble – If this is happiness
then count me in – New: 0172/three times four or Have
you prayed tonight? – I want more happiness... Now
relax: hope is half of life – Happiness... Not every day is
Sunday, and say: What want you with the dagger? – I
want happiness... A good person doesn't do that –
Happiness... Is laid to your charge – Happiness... You're
under arrest – Happiness...*rien ne va plus* my dear
Humour is laughter in the face of – The... Shut up.
(*He falls to the ground and lies motionless.*)

FELIX: And you know what I can't understand? (*Pause.*)
How your mother took the piece and put it on my plate.

ANNA: That was our last night as far as I'm concerned. I'll
put your things outside the door.

FELIX: (*Throws down his hat.*) Yes. Anyway it's all Romeo's
fault.
(*Thunder. Dark.*)

6. Love at first trick/Learning by doing II

*Midday. FELIX sits alone at the bar. HELMBRECHT is on his
stone again.*

FELIX: To Rudolf Valentino! (*He drinks.*) Rudolf Valentino's
a role model of mine. (*He drinks.*

ANNA runs in and sits at the bar, out of breath. She drinks.
Silence.)
You're back?

ANNA: The streets are empty. The sky's all black.
Everything looks so different.
(*Silence.*)
Felix?

FELIX: Yes.

ANNA: I'm putting the balldress on.

FELIX: What?

ANNA: Yes, we have to work!

FELIX: Now?

ANNA: Yes! There are two days to the revival. In theory.
I'm putting the balldress on and going on to the balcony.
Helmbrecht! We have to talk. Listen: You're in love!
You'd give all your bison. Top of the arm. Under the
arm. Breast touching. That's yesterday's news. You're
head over heels in love with me now. You have to have
me or die. (*She goes off. Silence.*
FELIX gives HELMBRECHT a script.)

FELIX: Yes. I mean: You like it Helogermanic? This is
right of the Rhine. Remember it. And you know what?
Her too. She's dying for it. Yes! Total abandon on both
sides! A human moment! No more air hugging! You can
smelt right away! How's that?
(*Silence.*)

HELMBRECHT: So soon?!

FELIX: What do you mean, so soon? That's how it is today.
Love goes fast. Now: Go and stand under the balcony!
(*FELIX directs the spotlight at the balcony.*
HELMBRECHT stands motionless.
FELIX invents further preparations.
*HELMBRECHT goes hesitantly, step by step, to stand under
the balcony.*
FELIX wraps himself in a scarf.
Then ANNA on the balcony in a ballgown.)
Good! Wait! I'll get my chair! (*He fetches his chair.*) So!
There's nothing to be gained from a part-swapping
improvisation in this case. We'll begin at: 'See! How she
leans her cheek upon her hand!' No. Let's skip that.

Straight to: 'O Romeo! Wherefore art thou Romeo?'
When you're ready.

ANNA: 'O Romeo! Wherefore art thou Romeo? Deny thy
father, and refuse thy name!'
(*Silence.*)

HELMBRECHT: Where's Romeo?

FELIX: – There! Under the balcony! Of course, I should
have said. You are now Romeo. You're standing under
the famous balcony, looking up. Again!

ANNA: 'O Romeo! Romeo! Wherefore art thou Romeo?
Deny thy father, and refuse thy name!'
(*Silence.*)

HELMBRECHT: (*Opens his mouth, and tries to speak, falters,
presses a hand to his temple – and then a soft, sad sound.*)

FELIX: Wrong speech. First comes: 'Shall I hear more, or
shall I speak at this?' Thank you.
(*Thunder.*)
God! I don't know what that constant sodding sound is
for! Quiet! (*Pause.*) So. 'Shall I hear more, or shall I
speak at this?' Thank you.

HELMBRECHT: I feel sick.

FELIX: Never mind. Again! And Anna: More focus. You're
too generalised. Thank you.

ANNA: (*Furious.*) 'O Romeo! Romeo! Wherefore art thou
Romeo? Deny thy father, and refuse thy name!'

FELIX: Stop! Anna! Not like that. You're in one of the most
moving moments known to humanity. Again.

ANNA: (*Still more furious.*) 'O Romeo! Romeo! Wherefore
art thou Romeo? Deny thy father, and refuse thy name!'
(*HELMBRECHT is sick in the fountain.*)

FELIX: (*Shouts.*) Anna! That's awful. I want linear sentences.
Sentences in which each thing follows from the one
before. Don't anticipate. Don't look back. No knots. You
need to thread the words like pearls on a string in the
English Romantic manner. Logical. Hierarchical.
Chronological. Psychological... –
(*ANNA just continues, transmuting as she does so her rage
against FELIX into an increasingly inflamed apparent passion
for HELMBRECHT.*)

ANNA: 'Tis but thy name that is my enemy;
      Thou art thyself though, not a Montague.
      What's in a name? that which we call a rose
      By any other name would smell as sweet;
      So Romeo would, were he not Romeo call'd,
      Retain that dear perfection which he owes
      Without that title. Romeo, doff thy name;
      And for that name, which is no part of thee,
      Take all myself!'
      (*HELMBRECHT has got up from the edge of the fountain
      and proceeds with increasing rapture to stand under the
      balcony. He wipes his mouth. He stares up at ANNA speechless,
      as if rooted to the spot. ANNA jumps to Act III Scene 5.*)
      'Wilt thou be gone? it is not yet near day;
      It was the nightingale, and not the lark,
      That pierced the fearful hollow of thine ear;
      Nightly he sings on yon pomegranate tree:
      Believe me, love, it was the nightingale.'
      (*Silence.*)

ROMEO: 'It was the lark, the herald of the morn,
      No nightingale: look, love, what envious streaks
      Do lace the severing clouds in yonder east...'
      (*FELIX presses a button on the remote control. Music. Perhaps
      Tchaikovsky's 'Fantastic Overture – Romeo and Juliet', mid-
      section. Best of all the DDR hit by Frank Schobel: 'Like a
      star in the summer night is love, as it starts to shine'. The
      music gets louder and louder and drowns out the actors, whose
      mouths noiselessly move to the power of the pearling words.
      Perhaps Romeo is saying: 'I have more care to stay than will
      to go' – when Juliet drops a handkerchief from the balcony
      and Romeo takes the handkerchief and runs it in his hands
      over his heart through his hair and up to heaven while throwing
      the exotic plants up to Juliet on the balcony one after another,
      and Juliet throws down more and more handkerchiefs to Romeo,
      whereupon Romeo throws first the cups and then all the coffee
      mugs up to Juliet, while the bubbling fountain springs ever
      higher and a sun in the background goes alternately up, golden
      and down, bloodred, so that no-one knows whether the lark
      or the nightingale is...until FELIX suddenly presses a button
      on the remote control. Silence. FELIX off.
      Dark.*)

7. All roads lead to Rome

Late afternoon. ANNA and ROMEO on the balcony.

ROMEO: It's beautiful. (*Silence.*) The head. And the heels. (*Pause.*) Anna?

ANNA: Yes.

ROMEO: Something's happening to me. Your face is changing. It's getting clearer. Brighter. It's become so I can understand it. (*Pause.*) Anna?

ANNA: Yes.

ROMEO: I was afraid before that our conversation might not be successful.
(*Silence.*)

ANNA: I was the same.

ROMEO: I feel so alive. I've forgotten all about Dietlinde. (*Pause.*) And also about what our conversation is supposed to be for.
(*FELIX comes in. He's carrying a coat and a sword. He sits in his chair.*)

ANNA: (*To ROMEO.*) Me too, I feel so alive inside. There's so much going on in my mind...

ROMEO: (*Looking at FELIX.*) Yes, that's right.

ANNA: It's suddenly clear to me, why in the beginning I experienced your face as being so closed. On one hand I was feeling such happiness inside – because of you. On the other hand, sadness in you – because of me? But that's gone now. I'm seeing eyes. I'm seeing your eyes. They're deep eyes. They're different from other people's eyes. You know? You think you can travel in behind people's eyes and then... (*FELIX gets up and goes.*)

ROMEO: That's beautiful. Would you like some coffee? Here! Take these blooms. There's so much that's new. Oh Anna, to think life used to be so closed. Do you see this stone? It was my best friend. Before, and on my way here. Take another bloom, you pink-and-blue life. We could have some chocolate now as well! (*He springs from the balcony.*) Anna?

ANNA: Yes.

ROMEO: Where is it? I mean: What does it look like?

ANNA: What?

ROMEO: The chocolate. Our chocolate for dinner.

ANNA: I don't want any chocolate at the moment.

ROMEO: Later perhaps?

ANNA: Yes, later perhaps.

ROMEO: I could sing something.

ANNA: No, don't sing anything. (*Pause.*) Tell me, before you came to this place. Where were you?

(*Silence.*)

Hullo?

(*ROMEO begins to move his head back and forth. He falters. Moves his lips. Takes a step forward and a step back. Holds a hand to his temple. Turns in a circle. Runs backwards towards his stone. Shyly raises an arm, on whose hand the fingers rise and fall. Briefly embraces the air. Then he breaks down. He stands motionless.*)

Are you not feeling well?

ROMEO: I don't know. I've forgotten.

ANNA: You've forgotten?

ROMEO: My mother's eyes. No. Dead. I still knew it before. The present. (*Pause.*) The present is so bright, I can't see the light at the other end any more. It's all become one thing.

(*Silence.*)

ANNA: Perhaps... (*Uneasy.*) – These things don't happen. Are you from Italy perhaps? Yes, perhaps you're Italian? As soon as we met, I immediately thought: Oh, an Italian! Then I thought: He's from Finland – or Lapland, because you were suddenly so withdrawn, and silent, and so turned in on yourself somehow thinking back on something. Then I thought: A Russian. Russians only really get going, when they've just had a shit or been sick. But now – you know – now I think: You're an Italian, from Italy. Those southern cheekbones. Listen. It's not so far away. Would you like to call home? I've got a telephone.

ROMEO: He had a dog. No. Was it the edge of the world? – I don't know. Once there were laws of the gods and the blades of the ploughshares. But why? An Italian from Italy?

ANNA: Yes, yes, that's right.
(*Silence.*)
ROMEO: A Roman from Rome?
ANNA: Rome?
ROMEO: We could ask Felix. He knows everything. He's my friend.
ANNA: I'm not so sure about that. Felix only loves himself. He only knows one person here, and that's himself.
ROMEO: But he greeted me.
ANNA: That doesn't mean anything.
ROMEO: Is he not your friend?
ANNA: No.
ROMEO: And you're not his friend?
ANNA: No.
ROMEO: But you came here because of him?
ANNA: I would have come here sooner or later anyway.
ROMEO: He was waiting for you.
ANNA: No he wasn't. Angela might just as easily have come.
ROMEO: Who's Angela?
ANNA: Another woman.
ROMEO: He knows another woman?
ANNA: I think he knows all the women there are.
ROMEO: But I thought the only person he knows is himself.
ANNA: The only person he sees in every woman is himself. All women are the same to him.
ROMEO: But I'm a man.
ANNA: Yes.
ROMEO: I'm his friend.
ANNA: No.
(*Silence.*)
ROMEO: But he is my friend. I'm going to call the first snowflake after him. (*Pause.*) Anna?
ANNA: Yes.
ROMEO: What shall we do now?
(*She smiles.*)
ANNA: Come on! I'll show you.
(*Dark.*)

THE THIRD DAY

8. Plans

Morning. ANNA and ROMEO wake up on the feather mattress. ROMEO climbs on to a chair.

ROMEO: Good morning. I should have someone walking in front of me, waving a white flag. Look at me! I've held my heart up to heaven. You have to let it fly for once, out from the cold walls. And if one person sees another one do it: Won't there be more and more in the world? Give me your shoes. I want to dance with you. I can already see so many people flying around, throwing their hearts into each other's arms. Anna. Isn't it recognition that moves people? I want so much to be in the world now. There! The sky's pink and blue, and real laughter is falling down on us. Shouldn't we get married? I'll work. I'll build a house for you, stone by stone. Do you like farmhouses? I'll build you a farmhouse in the middle of Bernsteinstrasse. We'll tell each other stories in the evening. We'll eat. We'll embrace the sunsets. Anna! (*He climbs down from the chair and embraces ANNA. He closes his eyes. Long pause. He opens his eyes again. Takes a step to the side. And now: he looks at ANNA.*) We've grown old.
ANNA: It was a beautiful time.
ROMEO: Yes. The farmhouse is still standing, just as on the first day.
ANNA: It was a beautiful time.
ROMEO: Yes. You said that.
(*Dark.*)

9. The womb is still fruitful...

ANNA and ROMEO sit on chairs facing each other. FELIX comes in with coat, sword and HELMBRECHT's helmet.

FELIX: Ouch! Right on the head! They've got baseball bats. What are you doing? I've been the whole night...
Where's my chair? I want my chair! Have you looked in

the refrigerator by any chance? There's only champagne
left in there. I want my breakfast! Where's my breakfast?
Romeo! Why are you staring at me like that? Fortunately
I was wearing this helmet.
(*ROMEO stands up.*
FELIX sits on his chair.)
ROMEO: We want to get married, Felix!
ANNA: Felix, you're bleeding. Give me the sword!
FELIX: What do you want?
(*She hurries to embrace him.*)
ANNA: My God. Darling. What's happened to your head?
FELIX: Oh for heaven's sake. A baseball bat, I already...
ROMEO: Do you know. If she were to die, she'd live in me,
not I.
FELIX: Shit. Bring me my breakfast, you idiot!
(*Silence.*)
ROMEO: No. (*Pause.*) I'll bring you champagne.
FELIX: You seem to think this all belongs to you! I'm not
your guest! Do I look like a guest? I can bring my own
breakfast. It can all be done without you. Sit here! Sit!
(*Pushes him on to his chair.*) Right! Watch this! I'll bring
you champagne! (*Off.*)
ROMEO: Anna. Your kiss made me understand the whole
world.
ANNA: I'm sorry, Romeo. This isn't Wagner. Can you do
this up. My hand is shaking.
ROMEO: Would you like us to swear by something?
ANNA: I don't know. Leave me alone. You're mad.
ROMEO: Do you think the gods will help us? It's a long
journey back there.
ANNA: I don't know. What journey? Where's Felix? He's
bleeding.
ROMEO: Don't you believe in our journey? Let's go. You
must... What do you believe in then?
ANNA: Heavens. I don't know. I...
ROMEO: Then have you never been in love before?
ANNA: God! I don't know that either. I can't do this. What
are you talking about?
(*FELIX enters.*)

ROMEO: Anna! Let's go! It was this kiss!

FELIX: Romeo?

(*Silence.*)

Come with me.

ANNA: Yes. Go. Please.

(*ROMEO off.*

ANNA stands motionless. Long pause. She takes her shoes. Runs through the room. Leans her head and back against the back wall. Closes her eyes. Opens them. Takes a step to the side. Spreads her arms. And then: she embraces the air. And moves on. She sits on the stone. Slowly puts her shoes on. Suddenly stands up. Runs to the fountain and looks at herself reflected in the water. Pause. She holds her face closer and closer to the water. Perhaps singing softly. Then she plunges in. Dark.)

10. The stranger is only strange in the rumour mill

Afternoon. ANNA and FELIX at the bar.

FELIX: I'll kill you if you and he…

(*Silence.*)

You're not serious.

ANNA: Just get the hairdryer. I need the hairdryer.

(*FELIX gets the hairdryer.*)

FELIX: So? Is he good?

(*She dries her hair.*)

ANNA: Amazing. Really amazing. Where is –

FELIX: The champagne?

ANNA: Romeo for heaven's sake!

FELIX: Right. In the fridge.

(*The dryer stops.*)

ANNA: Romeo is in the fridge?

FELIX: Yes, with the champagne. The fellow is simply unbearable.

(*She jumps up.*

He restrains her.)

ANNA: Look, have you gone mad? You can't just –

FELIX: What, the champagne?

(She smiles.)
ANNA: Romeo for heaven's sake.
(He smiles.)
FELIX: In the fridge.
ANNA: Romeo is in the fridge?
FELIX: Yes, with the champagne. The swine is simply
  unbearable.
(She jumps up.
He tenderly restrains her.)
ANNA: Have you gone mad? You can't just –
FELIX: What, the spaghetti-eater?
ANNA: Our foreign fellow-citizen for heaven's sake!
FELIX: Right. He's in the refrigerator as well. Our foreign
  fellow-citizen is simply unbearable.
ANNA: Have you gone mad? You can't just – in the
  refrigerator like that.
FELIX: What, that swine?
ANNA: For heaven's sake. Our asylum-seeking spaghetti-
  eater.
FELIX: Right. He's in the refrigerator as well. An asylum-
  seeking swine, who eats spaghetti, is simply unbearable.
ANNA: Have you gone mad? You can't just lock an HIV-
  positive, asylum-seeking spaghetti-eating swine in the
  fridge.
FELIX: Anna?
ANNA: Yes.
FELIX: Was it good?
ANNA: What, the champagne?
FELIX: Perhaps he'll die. He looks very thin.
ANNA: Yes he's certainly hungry.
FELIX: He looks Lebanese.
ANNA: I think he misses his mother.
FELIX: Just don't give him a diarrhoea pill. We'll all be
  blown sky high.
ANNA: He speaks a lot about God.
FELIX: Gottlieb Klopstock. I think he's a terrorist. Has he
  ever asked for a lotus plum?
ANNA: He's beyond boundaries. I believe he's broken free
  of something. You know the Grail?

FELIX: Of course. Richard Wagner. Sounds dangerous. He'll probably run amok.

ANNA: Felix?

FELIX: Yes.

ANNA: I think you should shave.

FELIX: Right.

ANNA: Do you know, I like him. You can ground yourself on him. With him, I feel I can play something that doesn't exist any more. And that's the difference. That's so beautiful. We ought to have a little celebration. In his honour. The golden newcomer. He's so alone. We ought to do something nice for him. Make a dream come true. Pink and blue, yes? Anything he wants. One night.

FELIX: Fine. First I have to show you something else. Then we'll get the champagne.

(*She dries her hair.*
Dark.)

11. Talking about women

Evening. Light on the fridge. Light on the stone. Then: voices.

STONE: Hullo. This is your stone. I've seen a lot of people in my time. Be careful. They're different. They vacillate.

ROMEO'S VOICE: You're speaking?

STONE: When I was lying with your parents at the bottom of the river I said to myself: if you ever see land again, you'll speak.

ROMEO'S VOICE: I brought you back among people. I carried you all the way here.

STONE: Thank you.

ROMEO'S VOICE: I leaned on you, you know, when my strength failed me. (*Pause.*) Do you like her?

STONE: Anna?

ROMEO'S VOICE: Yes.

STONE: Ah. I've seen a lot of women in my time. Be on your guard. She has a big pink-and-blue heart. But it's not the same as yours. It's black inside. And it's harder. She can't hold it up to the world and look through it as you can. Do you want her?

ROMEO'S VOICE: Yes! But something isn't right yet.

STONE: I have to speak more slowly. It's tiring when you haven't spoken for such a long time.

ROMEO'S VOICE: What can I do?

STONE: I don't want to say.

ROMEO'S VOICE: Say it!

STONE: You have to make your heart harder. It mustn't shoot into the sky at every opportunity. Ah. It's wonderful you can both fly. But here – here you have to know how to land. My God. I'm tired. I'll have to stop now.

ROMEO'S VOICE: But how can I make my heart harder?

STONE: Look at people! You haven't been looking properly.

ROMEO'S VOICE: Ah – I haven't been looking properly.

STONE: And another thing. She's living ahead of you. You'll have to go faster, for her to be able to run into your arms. You can't carry her through time like me. Farewell.

ROMEO'S VOICE: But how can I go faster here?
(*Silence.*)
Do I really have to stay here with her? Couldn't we just go back and see what things are like at home? – I planted a tree in our woods.
(*Silence.*)
You know, I could take you back with me? (*Pause.*) You know Bernsteinstrasse?
(*Silence.*)
Hullo? (*Pause.*) It's a very nice street. (*Pause.*) Bernsteinstrasse. (*Pause.*) Good night.
(*Dark.*)

12. Invited to supper

It's still evening. Table laid. Chocolate. Coffee. Champagne. Remains of cocktails. FELIX is leaning against the wall. ANNA is folding table napkins.

ANNA: Felix?

FELIX: Yes.

ANNA: Sometimes you're really...

FELIX: ...strong?

ANNA: No. The opposite.

FELIX: Weak?

ANNA: Yes. But now you're in the middle.

FELIX: The middle of the two opposites?

ANNA: Yes. Balanced.

FELIX: Middling weak!

ANNA: Exactly.

FELIX: Is that good?

ANNA: Yes. Very!

FELIX: Good. To us! (*He drinks.*)

ANNA: Stop. You know how you're actually drinking?

FELIX: How I'm actually drinking?

ANNA: Yes. Like Robert de Niro. It's that inevitability in
your outline. It's much too strong. You could let it go.

FELIX: Fine. – Anna?

ANNA: Yes.

FELIX: Watch. (*He drinks.*)

ANNA: Yes. That's it. Also it suits you much better.

FELIX: Thank you.

ANNA: Don't mention it. (*Pause.*) Felix?

FELIX: Yes.

ANNA: Where's –

FELIX: The champagne?

ANNA: Oh no stop it. Romeo.
    (*Silence.*)

FELIX: Anna?

ANNA: Yes.

FELIX: Has this ever happened to you? You've got an
appointment, but you can't remember who with.
Recently for example. I had an appointment for ten past
five. But I just didn't know any more, who it was with.
I'd made the appointment when I was on one escalator,
with someone coming towards me on the other escalator.
At the airport. Yes. And of course I immediately realised
there were lots of people who'd been coming towards me
on the other escalator that I might in theory have made
an appointment with.
(*ANNA is lighting candles.*)

Listen. So I decided it would be best if I divided people into two categories. First, category one: people I knew very well – from seeing them, I mean: from the way they looked – but I'd never spoken to. Then category two: people I'd spoken to, but in principle I didn't know them at all, and therefore I didn't see them at all, like Peter for example, who was also on the escalator... Anna?

ANNA: Yes?

FELIX: Are you listening to me?

ANNA: I think we're ready.

FELIX: Good. Yes. Fine. Eat, stranger, of the servants' food. Odyssey. Fourteenth song. (*He opens the refrigerator.*) We invite you in the name of the republic to take your place at the festive table!

(*FELIX presses the remote control. From the music box is heard Verdi's 'Triumphal March', or the prisoners' chorus from Nabucco. ROMEO emerges from the fridge. Completely frozen as is natural. He moves very slowly forwards and stands motionless at the table.*)

Revered Mr President. A small piece of advice. If you're about to embark on another political speech: Put your hands over your crotch. A tiny change, but it makes a big difference.

ANNA: Felix, excuse me! I didn't mean like this. What I meant was, be really nice, yes? Just listen to yourself: first he's Romeo. Now he's suddenly the President. Tell me, are you crazy: he was really in the refrigerator! It can't be more than two above zero! What are you trying to do to him?

FELIX: Why me? He started it. He just walked in here as if he were Hölderlin. And where does it say for example that Shakespeare's Juliet was in love with a Hun... I mean...

ROMEO: I'm so cold.

(*Silence.*)

How can flowers bloom here? I'm sorry – Are we getting married? (*Stretches out a hand to ANNA.*)

FELIX: Not now. You've suddenly been selected by the management. And we approved it. Between ourselves: it will also be seen by the outside world as an important gesture of rapprochement. So: you'll still be coming in from upstage. Walk downstage, upright but loose – like Rudolf Valentino! A personal role model of mine. A brief wave to either side. Then the hands straight over the crotch. Then the speech. Thank you.

(*Silence.*)

Rudolf Valentino? Of course. I should have said. Well: Rudolf Valentino basically walked like this. (*He walks about like that.*) And anyway, that's a professional walk. Yes, in professional walking, everything depends on the flexibility of knees, hips and head. (*He walks about again.*)

ANNA: Excuse me. Maybe that's how Gottlieb Klopstock walks. But not Rudolf Valentino. Valentino walks like this. (*She, too, walks about.*) Knees, hips and head – yes of course. But you have to join them up. It comes from a kind of soft but powerful interaction of horizontal and vertical movements. Which means: you counterbalance the knee-head axis by swinging the hips. I'll do it again. (*She does it again.*)

FELIX: You know. I think your problem is, you do too much. You can walk, but when you just have to stand on the balcony, awful.

(*ANNA laughs.*)

ANNA: You arsehole. Perform your stupid balcony scene yourself.

(*Silence.*)

ROMEO: I'm sorry. I... I'll walk now.

(*Silence.*)

FELIX: Oh yes. Please.

ANNA: My poor cold prince. Here. Take this coat and tell us one of your beautiful dreams. I love your dreams. (*She places the coat on his shoulders. He walks upstage and back in a mixture of Gottlieb Klopstock and Rudolf Valentino. Waves briefly to either side then places his hands over his crotch. Then: he speaks without making any sound.*)

FELIX: Excuse me. A bit clearer if possible.

(*ROMEO again begins moving his head gently back and forth. At the same time he raises first one, and then the other, hand, the fingers rising and falling in front of his torso, until he drops his arms. Then he stands motionless.*)

ROMEO: He... Once there was... I can't do it any more. I want to speak from my heart, but only my lips are moving.

FELIX: Then speak with your lips.

ROMEO: Just the lips?

FELIX: Exactly.

ANNA: You haven't got the faintest idea what he's talking about.

FELIX: Aha. And quiet please.

(*Silence.*)

PRESIDENT: Bla-bla. Bla-bla. Dear esteemed bison. Centuries have passed, since you were last called together, as you are today, in such numbers and on a matter of such urgency to all of us. Foreign herds have crossed our national borders and established themselves in our wood- and meadowland plains. They say: They're just here for dessert. But in reality they're grazing us to the ground. They're eating the food intended for tomorrow, and for the day after, and my head spins, when I walk the meadows of an evening. I recently invited one of their principal leaders to my office. I said to him: Bla-bla. It won't do. If everyone continues to graze like this, there'll be no grazing left for anyone. He said: Bla-bla. Let's make an agreement. I said: Good. Work yes, grazing no. He said: How can that be? It would be better if: Everyone graze. And when there's no more left to graze, the weak can be grazed upon by the strong – which is you. I said: Correct. That's life. We'll permit you to graze, only in order that you'll be strong enough to produce goods and that you won't be thin, when we finally throw off our sheep's clothing and... He said: So we'll all live semi-happily together till the time comes and you... Yes, till we strip off your fat and... And our blood and our hides... And throw your remains in the fire... And you'll survive... Correct: And we'll take all your goods... And we'll be dead, or, vice versa... Bla-bla: How do you mean, vice versa?... Bla-bla: because there are going to be a lot of us, when the time comes... Anna, what am I talking about?

(*Thunder like a bomb exploding in the distance. They eat chocolate. In blocks. Edelbitter.*
Dark.)

13. Monologue for two I

Night. ROMEO sits by his stone.

ROMEO: Hullo? – I can't sleep. I'm having such bad dreams. What about you? Do you sleep? Can you dream?
(*Silence.*)
Why won't you answer me? You have to answer me! Do you know Peter? Is Valentino good? Do you like Felix? He saved me, did he? But what about his hand in my face... Do you know? (*Pause.*) Listen. She said: home! Wake up. Where is home? Hullo? Who's Valentino?
(*Silence.*)
Watch. Am I good at walking? (*He walks around the stone.*) Do I walk well? – Watch! I want to get the style. I don't want to walk like Gottfried Klopstock. I'm going to counterbalance my axis from now on. – But you: you've got boring. You're not even looking! Did you hear? I have beautiful dreams! She loves my dreams. Did you see me kiss her? I held her in my arms. Look! She gave me this coat. I'm a prince. What's a cold prince? How does a cold prince dream? Can you hear? You should answer me. (*He lies on the stone.*) Are you talking very quietly? (*Pause.*) I'll put my ear to you. (*Pause.*) You're silent. All of time is contained in you. And you? (*Pause.*) You're silent. (*He falls asleep.*
Dark.)

14. Night pictures I

Red dream light on the balcony. ANNA above. FELIX with hat below. And now: She falls down into his arms. He holds her. She embraces him. He twirls her. She takes the hat. He twirls her faster. Dancing. Then kissing. Flowers everywhere. And soft laughter growing ever louder, terminating on a shrill high point.

Dark.

15. Monologue for two II

The same night. ROMEO starts up.

ROMEO: What's that? Where's it going? Now here, now there. Weren't we going to dance? Are kisses so meaningless? – My head. Where's my head? (*Sinks back on to his stone.*) I wanted to talk with you about truth. But you're not talking. You're silent. (*Pause.*) Be silent then. I'm not going to carry you through time any more – no. It's so dark. It's as if the night were crying out of the darkness. Goodbye. I swore to her in tears. (*Dark.*)

16. Night pictures II

ANNA dances with ROMEO. Pink and blue dream light. Soft piano music.

ANNA'S VOICE: Do you know? I can go in behind your eyes and then: Then there's a ballroom, and roses and music and through the doors which are open like wings, the wind blows in from a lake and on it are the white sails of ships coming towards the land, shining pink and blue beyond the water. My saviour. My beautiful vision! Is it so far? Where's your street? How far does my life reach? – Let's go. Take my shoes. Carry me through the rooms to the other side of the storms. Can you hear the blood rushing? How easy it was to give up stupid old reason. Let's go! In your arms. Come. My love. Let's end it all or go. (*Dark.*)

THE FOURTH DAY

17. You have to blow your own trumpet

The next morning. ROMEO wakes up on his stone. Stares at the mattress: ANNA is lying in FELIX's arms. She gets up. Pulls on the balldress. Goes to the bar. ROMEO follows. She drinks.

ROMEO: Now here! Now there! I think... Good morning. Shall I do that up? The...

ANNA: Don't.

ROMEO: Why isn't your hand shaking?
(*She drinks.*)
French Connection is good.

ANNA: No Southern Comfort. Enjoy your breakfast. (*Pause.*) Romeo. I'm... I don't know.

ROMEO: (*Quietly.*) Southern Comfort is Manhattan Dry. (*He drinks five French Connections straight down.*)
Let's go!
(*She drinks.*)
Now here! Now there! Anna. We could go away from here. Do you know where? (*Pause.*) You know. Because I... Hullo? (*He seizes her.*)

ANNA: 'Just touch me, Franz! I'd rather have a knife in my body than your hand on mine.'

FELIX: (*Lying on the mattress.*) Anna. Excuse me. That's a different play. (*To ROMEO.*) Do you know: She always wants to play Lulu and Marie and Juliet all at once.

ROMEO: Anna! I... What? What is this? Where is it – the land behind the eyes? (*Pause.*) Anna? Can't you come? (*She drinks. Silence. He holds first one hand, then the other, flat against his temples. He stops the seeking movements and hits himself on the back of the head. Pause. It's as if he now has to bring himself to do something. A dive. Or a hundred metre run. He takes a deep breath.*)
I... I introduced a new circumstance into you, and what was there before is yesterday's news. Look into my eyes and don't interrupt me. It could just as well have been Angela who came. Now take off the balldress. Who would weep, if appetite grows by what it feeds on. Perhaps

you're from Italy. I have a telephone. Hullo? – Anna?
So how much does a heart have to weigh these days?
How many colours does it have to have? And how many
eyes are there in a face like that? Can I run from both
sides in one direction? I... I have a telephone. I want
linear sentences. No knots. There's no ice. Aren't you
well? Take off the balldress. We have to work.
(*ANNA takes off the balldress.*
FELIX directs the spotlight on to the stage.
ROMEO drinks.)
Good. You didn't like your last mouthful of cordon bleu.
But how could you scream and spit it on your mother's
plate? I'm not your guest... Anna? – Don't you know
where? I know where. I told... (*He drinks.*) – You're too
generalised. Whether you think democracy's a good
form of government? I have a telephone. Hullo? You've
all gone mad. And put on the balldress. That's how it is
these days. Love goes fast. Come on, I'll show you.
What's in a name? That which we call a rose by any
other name would smell as sweet: so Romeo would, were
he not Romeo called. – Anna, my head! Hold my head.
Am I Peter now? What does a president do? Tell me! Is
that my saviour? Anna! If everything would just be quiet
for once. You know! I dreamt about it! The land, free,
and how to get back to it. Do you hear? But how fast do
I have to run here? Do you hear me? – And put on the
balldress. Her. Me. You. You'd made a date with both
women without thinking.
(*ANNA puts on the balldress. FELIX sits on his chair. He*
applauds. ROMEO drinks.)
On one hand I felt such joy in me because of you. On
the other hand. Haven't you got any mineral water?
I want breakfast. And what shall I do? Weak. Strong.
Strong. Weak. Wrong speech. First comes: Anna! But I
told... Weren't we both at that film? I... I wish I'd grown
up somewhere else! I'd have made a big festival in your
honour! Do you hear me? Give me your shoes. I want to
dance with you... No more air hugging. Do you hear me?
(*Silence.*)
Fine.

(*He seizes the stone. Runs with the stone through the back wall. Flickering light comes in.*)
So. I'll make bombs. Bombs are science. And in addition. Hope as the construction of a Point B, when Point A has become unendurable. It can't be more than two above zero. I'm dying! Bang! Did you sleep with him? Thank you! I would have come here in any case. But where's the beauty we keep talking about?
(*Thunder. ROMEO now walks about. He forces himself more and more into being grotesquely loose, in order to fight his tears. He contradicts the knee-head axis by swinging his hips. Thunder. He runs to the telephone. He dials.*)
Swam across. My name is Valentino. My friends are far away. Can you hear me? All I've got is what I stand up in... I have a telephone. Hullo, hullo? Should I speak? Thank you. I've fallen out of the nest. No reason. My greetings to nobody. Stop.
(*Thunder. ROMEO drops the receiver and staggers off. At the same time FELIX jumps up from his chair and runs through the room.*)

FELIX: Shit! I'd so love to live in the country. To be looking into the distance right now! Can you hear the wind in the trees? I want sunsets. A bit of red sky. And in the mornings, watching the summer climb up out of the depths. Let's run through the mist across the fields!
(*Thunder.*)
Once and for all, turn that noise off! We could fetch our own milk and bread. I'd like to grow basil. It's wonderfully quiet on the roads. Anna. So where shall we live? Let's take each day as it comes. Where's my chair? Can't we just look at each other for once with no reason? Anna! It's got so dark all of a sudden in front of my eyes! I need my chair!
(*Loud thunder. Dark.*)

18. To be or not to be

Midday. FELIX is sitting in his chair, staring through the hole in the wall. Sunbeams shine through. ANNA is looking at herself in the water of the fountain.

ANNA: There are times when he's really irritating. He's changed so much. The way he suddenly comes out with those fundamental explanations of his. His overpowering wanting-it-all-right-now, and at the slightest obstacle he... I find it very un-erotic. (*She holds her face right near the surface of the water.*) You know. I sometimes think I've been put together out of nothing but rags and scraps, I'm just a patchwork, and every moment, every scrap is playing its own different game. There's as much difference between me and me as there is between me and you. Can you understand it?

FELIX: Of course. Look. The weather's got much nicer recently. See the sunbeams?

ANNA: On the other hand sometimes you're so close to me, and then I think a lot of the different scraps might be from you. And I can still see a difference between me and me but I can't any longer see any difference between me and you. (*Pause.*) Felix?

FELIX: Yes.

ANNA: Assuming you feel the same thing: then the two of us together are at least four people in one.
(*Silence.*)
And if you feel there's some third person between you and you, as I do between me and me: Then we'd be six. In one! Amazing.

FELIX: Anna?

ANNA: Yes.

FELIX: You'll find the binoculars beside the refrigerator. Come over here with the binoculars.
(*ANNA comes with the binoculars.*
FELIX looks through the binoculars.)

ANNA: Last night I saw the world burning.
(*Silence.*)
When I looked to the very end I could see a young man. He wanted to bring me my shoes, but suddenly he was in flames, and all I could see was...

FELIX: My God! Come here!
(*They look together through the hole in the wall.*)
Can you see that?

ANNA: What? The fire?

FELIX: No. The man. In between.

ANNA: Do you know him?

FELIX: He looks so familiar.

ANNA: Yes.

FELIX: And the cows?

ANNA: Why has he got cows on leads when it's universal chaos?

FELIX: I don't know either.

ANNA: Felix?

FELIX: Yes?

ANNA: He's so far away.

FELIX: Yes.

ANNA: So why can I hear him singing?

FELIX: Singing?

ANNA: Yes.

FELIX: You're right. I can hear it now. He's singing. (*Pause.*) Anna?

ANNA: Yes?

FELIX: He's embracing the cows.
(*Silence.*)

ANNA: I think he's turning round.

FELIX: He's turning round?

ANNA: Yes!

FELIX: Where to?

ANNA: Straight towards us! He'll be here in a minute!
(*Thunder.*)

FELIX: Anna?

ANNA: Yes.

FELIX: I'm going to switch off that sound now.
(*VALENTINO enters, very loose, with a hat.*)

VALENTINO: Excuse me. Where's Helmbrecht?
(*Dark.*)

19. Madness. Method. Quartet

ANNA. FELIX. VALENTINO. All at the bar.

ANNA: Helmbrecht?

VALENTINO: Yes.
(*Silence.*)

FELIX: You can't be asking us where Helmbrecht is?
(*Silence.*)
Don't you find that a bit strange? I mean: why are you
asking, when you... Do you know him?
VALENTINO: Yes. But not well.
FELIX: And what do you think of him?
VALENTINO: Stupid.
ANNA: But he isn't stupid! (*ANNA takes a step towards
VALENTINO.*) I think he's lovely. He's held his heart up
to heaven. He can embrace a thought.
FELIX: You must like something about him?
(*Silence.*)
You know, he thinks very well of people.
(*ANNA takes another step towards VALENTINO.*)
ANNA: There really are such people. They look at you, and
you immediately feel inwardly strong.
FELIX: At a time when utopias are completely out of
fashion, a person like him is an incredible stroke of luck.
ANNA: And he used to have a stone for a friend. Imagine.
FELIX: He treats a stone exactly like a snowflake or dog.
(*ANNA is now standing in front of VALENTINO.*)
ANNA: Yes, that's right. What dog?
FELIX: He had a dog. It died.
ANNA: I think his mother died too.
FELIX: And his father. They drowned themselves together.
With the stone.
ANNA: My God. Where? In Italy?
FELIX: In the Rhine. On the right hand side. Under the
black sky. His mother had buttered bread for him at
sunrise. When he woke up, she was gone. There was only
the bread and butter. A whole table full.
(*ANNA is walking backwards away from VALENTINO.*)
ANNA: So how does he have this love of life? He wanted to
build me a farmhouse in the middle of Bernsteinstrasse.
(*Silence.*)
FELIX: You know, the greatest drama about him is: he's
never yet known woman's nakedness.
(*Silence.*)
ANNA: (*Quietly.*) Are you sure?
(*Silence.*)

FELIX: What do you want with him?

VALENTINO: There's something I have to say to him.

FELIX: What do you want to say to him?

VALENTINO: It's a secret.

(*Silence.*)

FELIX: Aha. Yes. I mean... (*Pause.*) – And so who are you?

VALENTINO: I told you. Valentino. I'm responsible for all this.

(*Thunder. Twice.*
VALENTINO off.
Dark.)

20. Goodbye stranger

Afternoon. FELIX is sitting on HELMBRECHT's stone.
VALENTINO is leaning on the bar. With hat. And scarf. He gives
the impression of a man who never loses his reserve. ANNA stands
with her back to the wall. Salon music is softly playing.

ANNA: So what are we, a shit factory? I've absolutely no idea why I'm taking part in this rubbish. Do you know what you haven't got? A concept. You have absolutely no idea. Of anything. When I look at you just sitting there! Four days! Perhaps you should just think about whether we might at some point do something. I mean: couldn't you just take your heads in your hands and wring out a little bit of brainpower for the world?

VALENTINO: Excuse me, what time is it?

ANNA: I beg your pardon?

VALENTINO: I said: What time is it?

ANNA: Just after five.

VALENTINO: Seventeen ten. I've no more time. You realize there are people who know how to do a thing like this. Take a look in my diary. More coffee? No thanks. A man in my position, you know. I get up just after five in the morning without fail. I'm never finished till ten seventeen in the evening. My job is reversing solidification. Valentino's smelting systems. Nationwide. Here's my card: crystalline with amorphous. Pink-and-blue with black. We smelt everything with everything – Did you say seventeen ten?

(*Silence.*)

ANNA: Do you understand this?

FELIX: No I don't think so.

ANNA: Nor do I. It's all horrible.

FELIX: It's like in the beginning. He was trying things then.

ANNA: Like Hölderlin. Yes I know.

FELIX: Now he's going more in the direction of Rockefeller. Listen. Is today really Thursday? The day of the revival? Theoretically! What's the time?

ANNA: Seventeen ten.

VALENTINO: So. Seventeen ten. I have an appointment.

FELIX: That's interesting. He has an appointment. Do you know who it's with?

VALENTINO: Yes.

FELIX: Who?

VALENTINO: Romeo.

(*Silence.*)

FELIX: Say something.

ANNA: What am I supposed to say?

FELIX: Something. Try.

ANNA: I think. You have an appointment with Helmbrecht.

VALENTINO: No. He's gone. I'm no longer in contact with Helmbrecht. That's why I have an appointment with Romeo. He knows where he is.

(*ANNA circles VALENTINO one last time. Then she gradually moves away. She sits on the stone.*)

ANNA: If you see Romeo, please tell him to give my regards to Helmbrecht. I miss him. He used to be such a clear person.

VALENTINO: Yes, give him my regards as well.

(*Silence.*)

FELIX: (*Quietly.*) Romeo has to give Helmbrecht Valentino's regards. God –

ANNA: Basically I liked him much better than Romeo.

(*Silence.*)

FELIX: Romeo is quite an ordinary person. No wonder you're meeting him. You meet them all over the place.

(*Machine gun fire.*)

VALENTINO: I have to go now. Good night. (*He gives ANNA a flower.*) Farewell. (*He leaves. Dark.*)

21. The World is Out of Joint

Evening. ANNA and FELIX at the bar. Flickering light falls through the hole in the wall.

FELIX: Watch this. (*He drinks.*) I feel this increasing desire for reference-free drinks. (*Drinks.*) I'm drinking and in doing so I'm more and more establishing my own au-then-ticity. I've got you to thank for that.

ANNA: Felix! We might have to stop this some time. We might have underestimated the situation.

FELIX: No. That sort of thing can't happen here. It happens in other places. Not here, Anna. We're safe here. What time is it?
(*Machine gun fire. FELIX runs to the hole in the wall.*)
Anna?

ANNA: Yes!

FELIX: Everything seems so unreal to me. It's as if I were looking at a picture. You know?

ANNA: What?

FELIX: You're looking at a picture, but all that's in your mind is: Damn! They should have focused the camera better.
(*Loud thunder.*
PETER rushes in. He is dressed like FELIX. He sinks on to the chair, out of breath.)

PETER: You're here! What an original place to be! We've been searching for you for days. Have you turned on the television? We're all in Goethestrasse. How are you? How on earth did you manage to break through?
(*Machine gun fire getting closer.*)

22. Apocalypse Now

A spotlight trained on the balcony. ANNA is above. PETER below.
FELIX with scarf on his chair.

ANNA: 'O Romeo! Romeo! Wherefore art thou Romeo?
  Deny thy father, and refuse thy name.
  What's in a name? That which we call a rose
  By any other name would smell as sweet;
  So Romeo would, were he not Romeo called,
  Retain that dear perfection which he owes
  Without that title. Romeo, doff thy name.'
  (*Approaching machine gun fire.*)
  'Wilt thou be gone? It is not yet near day.
  It was the nightingale, and not the lark,
  That pierc'd the fearful hollow of thine ear;
  Nightly she sings on yon pomegranate tree:
  Believe me, love, it was the nightingale.'
  (*Plaster falls from the ceiling.*)
PETER: 'It was the lark, the herald of the morn,
  No nightingale: look, love, what envious streaks
  Do lace the severing clouds in yonder east...'
  (*FELIX presses the remote control. Music sounds. It grows*
  louder and drowns out the performers, whose mouths continue
  to move to the power of the pearling words. Perhaps PETER
  is just saying: 'I have more care to stay than will to go' as the
  machine gun fire draws ever nearer. More thunder. More
  and more plaster falling from the ceiling. ANNA throws
  handkerchiefs to PETER. PETER throws the exotic blooms to
  ANNA. Spotlights tumble from above. ANNA declaims.
  Machine gun fire. Richard Wagner. The wall slowly breaks
  around the hole. PETER raises his arms to heaven. Parts of
  the ceiling fall down. FELIX sits on his chair. It thunders.
  Twice. Three times. Marching footsteps. Lightning from outside.
  Now: A man like a cross in the break in the wall. It thunders.
  Four times. Five times. ANNA clutches at the balcony. The
  music centre jumps. Triumphal March. Götterdämmerung.
  Götterdämmerung. Triumphal March. And then. Machine
  gun fire in the room. PETER falls to his knees. The man in
  the hole in the wall: lowers his weapon. Lightning. Footsteps.

Thunder. PETER sinks to the ground. ANNA jumps down from the balcony. FELIX sits motionless on his chair. The fountain runs dry. The music ends. ANNA bends down over PETER.)

ANNA: Peter?

(*Silence.*)

He's dead. See the blood? He's dead!

(*The MAN climbs through the hole into the room. He is wrapped in white linen and barefoot. He wears a helmet. He walks slowly towards ANNA.*)

ANNA: Felix. I think... my God...

(*FELIX sits motionless in his chair. The YOUNG MAN IN LINEN seizes the stone. He goes slowly up to ANNA. She kneels. He stands in front of her. She looks up. He lifts the stone higher. She reaches out her shoes to him.*)

ANNA: No... Come...

(*The stone – breaks. Silence.*

The YOUNG MAN IN LINEN drags PETER's body through the room and into the refrigerator.

FELIX sits motionless in his chair.

The MAN IN LINEN picks ANNA up. He goes to the wall. Complete silence.)

HELMBRECHT: Anna! Look – the path. The end of the path. Sunset! See it? We'll embrace the sunset at the end – Anna.

(*HELMBRECHT goes out through the hole in the wall towards the setting sun.*

Dark.)

23. Felix

FELIX sits motionless in his chair. He has plaster all over his hair and body. He stands up. He walks slowly over to Anna's shoes. He picks them up. He holds them. It is silent. A YOUNG WOMAN runs in. She is out of breath.

THE YOUNG WOMAN: I ran and ran. Where are the others? It's like something I saw in the cinema. And you? My feet... Is that my balldress? – What happened here?

(*Silence.*)

FELIX: Hullo, Angela.

ANGELA: Have you got anything to drink?

FELIX: In the refrigerator. Champagne. If you want.

(*She goes to the refrigerator.*
He sinks down on his stone.
Dark.)

The End.

WARWESER

(Maienschlager)

I wish to thank Katharina Gericke, David Lan and Andreas Beck as well as everyone at the Goethe Institute, the Royal Court and Oberon Books for their support and encouragement in completing this translation.

Characters

MARK WARWESER (16)

JAKOB GLÜCKSLEBEN (15)

VIOLA WARWESER
WILLO WARWESER
Mark's parents, owners of a photo salon

REBEKKA GLÜCKSLEBEN
JAKOB GLÜCKSLEBEN SENIOR
Jakob's parents, grocers

SONJA
a barmaid

PETER HUNDT
KRISTA
Mark's classmates

YOUNG MAN WITH SQUINT

PIMPF

DR EHRLICHER
RABBI SÜSS
from the former Jewish temple

MAN IN OVERCOAT

SS MAN

In the Prologue:

MAN 1
MAN 2

Location
The area around the Goetheplatz in Nowawes between
Potsdam and Berlin

Period
1938, May/June, September-November
(Prologue: Summer 1954)

Setting
As far as possible the stage should be bare except for
whatever object determines that specific scene
(bed, tree, cross etc.)

~

This translation of *Warweser* was first performed as a rehearsed
reading on 13 November 1999 at The Royal Court Theatre,
London, with the following cast:

VIOLA, Annette Badland
SONJA, Eve Best
PIMPF, Darren Cheek
MARK, Matthew Dunster
MAN WITH SQUINT/DR EHRLICHER, Sean Gilder
PETER, Stuart Goodwin
WILLO/SS MAN, Paul Jesson
KRISTA, Pauline Lynch
REBEKKA, Catherine Purcell
JAKOB, Andrew Scott
JAKOB SNR/RABBI/MAN WITH OVERCOAT,
                                    Philip Whitchurch

Director, David Lan
Stage Manager, Julie Sproule

Prologue

Adriatic. A rocky beach in Montenegro.

MAN 1: Now we're just a grave and a headstone.

MAN 2: How did you find me here? The path over the crags is dangerous. Those rocks are sharp. You've torn the straps on your sandals.

MAN 1: Doesn't matter. I was following you.

MAN 2: You've been following me the whole time I've been here! Blocking out the sun on the hotel terrace with your intimidatingly wide shadow. My wife's scared of you and the children call you the stupid German doctor. Fear and desire trembling in their voices...

MAN 1: You can tell your little monsters if they draw any more pictures of me in the sand I'll give them a nasty injection... I really am a doctor. State or private...

MAN 2: No beard...

MAN 1: I knew it!

MAN 2: You'd be better off saving your attention for the beautiful young lady you're with!

MAN 1: My sister. I sent her out dancing tonight. Let her dance with those Yugoslav boys! She's young.

MAN 2: My wife's putting the children to bed. Afterwards we'll stay in the hotel foyer and eat all the grapes out of the fruit bowl... Till even you've gone dancing!

MAN 1: Dancing?! Me?! In that Tivoli-thing there? The nightlife in Montenegro is... If only I could sleep...

MAN 2: We're in the next room...

MAN 1: With your children crying all night long!

MAN 2: That's the sort of children I've got.

MAN 1: How's anyone next door supposed to sleep with your children howling and screaming all the time?!

MAN 2: They just can't take the heat here – at night. They've been bitten by mosquitoes then scratch the bites till they bleed. The repellent we've got's useless. If you want to complain, complain to the manager. Not me.

MAN 1: We could go to the bar on the point with the sea on three sides and have a Jim Beam.

MAN 2: Jim Beam? And I have to spend the whole time arguing with unmarried aesthetes who can't stand the sound of children.

MAN 1: Come on! Don't forget your newspapers, there on the rock. You read a lot of languages...

MAN 2: I have to. I'm a journalist in Brussels... Not Palestine...

MAN 1: I knew it!

MAN 2: Weird – the way the night falls so abruptly...like the moment of death...

MAN 1: Weird – the way the music in the bar starts so abruptly. The oldie of the moment being played for the thousandth time, my favourite...

MAN 2: I thought it annoyed you...

MAN 1: Not if you're with me...

MAN 2: Don't!

MAN 1: Don't – don't spoil this song for me.

MAN 2: 'It Happened in May.' A slow foxtrot... You're not dancing with me!

MAN 1: Oh... because of the children... We're leaving first thing tomorrow.

MAN 2: Thanks.

MAN 1: Don't be frightened....

MAN 2: Stop crying on my shoulder!

MAN 1: It's the last night of the holiday... Are you frightened I might say too much...after midnight... around three...the red sun rises over Capri, and you can see the sea on three sides, the waves spit foam at the rocks...all white...and then pink in the light. My story begins with the Hitler[1] salute.

PART ONE

Scene 1

Meeting. May 1938

Morning, outside Warweser's house.

PIMPF: (*Arm raised.*) Heil Hitler, Warweser!

MARK: Is that meant to be a salute?! What kind of salute's that?! Button your sleeves up, a German boy does not show his forearms in May! Is that how you stand to attention in front of Warweser, you call that standing to attention? Your feet are all over the place, and your cheeks, you little shit, pull 'em together! Chest out, stomach in, chin up, chin up! (*Shouting.*) I want you polishing for three hours before breakfast in future, and if that doesn't make you any better I'll have you doing drill here in the square – crawl, up, down, up, down! Now how do you salute Warweser?

PIMPF: (*Arm raised.*) Heil Hitler, Warweser!

MARK: There's a job you can do for me, you little twerp. Give Krista this love letter, just hand it to her as you go past…got it? (*Shouting.*) What are you waiting for?

PIMPF: Sorry, which one's Krista?

MARK:Which one do you think? The tallest one, the best-looking… Piss off!

(*PIMPF disappears.*)

MAN WITH SQUINT: You've got the Youth[2] organised, no-one wastes a minute, very good.

MARK: (*Arm raised.*) Heil Hitler, Jungsturmmann!

MAN WITH SQUINT: We-ll…?

MARK: Heil Hitler, Jungsturmmann!

MAN WITH SQUINT: That'll do. Got to go. The kiddies down there are fighting again.

MARK: Mr Meier the head teacher likes a few bloody noses in the rosy glow first thing.

MAN WITH SQUINT: It won't do, kiddies with bloody noses before school even starts.

MARK: Of course.

MAN WITH SQUINT: There's no smoking at the leadership college at Bad Berka.

MARK: A German boy does not smoke.

MAN WITH SQUINT: You still seeing the whore?

MARK: What whore?

MAN WITH SQUINT: That slag Sonja.

MARK: Beg your pardon but I disagree.

MAN WITH SQUINT: What's that supposed to mean?!

MARK: If I'm going to fight the fight to rid the world of Untermenschen – beg your pardon comrade – I've got to find out about them!

MAN WITH SQUINT: Very good! Comrade Grohmann'll put your name forward for the leadership college at Bad Berka.

MARK: I'd love to go there!

MAN WITH SQUINT: You would?

MARK: I would. Everything's right in my world, right, right, right...

KRISTA: Thanks for your note, Mark Warweser. My first love letter.

MARK: My pleasure.

KRISTA: That May dance...weren't we the picture of spring the two of us under the Führer's portrait! You ladling pea soup into my mess-tin... All the coloured streamers, idyllic it was. Dancing to old folk tunes as the German sun set scarlet in the German sky...

MAN WITH SQUINT: You've got to feel her minge, her minge... Have you felt her minge yet?

MARK: All in good time.

(*KRISTA giggles, runs away.*)

MAN WITH SQUINT: The desire to breed, it's healthy, I always say. National Socialism gives girls red cheeks and strong calves. Under the Führer they're all happy as larks. (*Exit.*)

SONJA: (*Enters.*) Don't throw your books away, Mark, it'd be such a waste...

MARK: Only just going home now, Sonja?

SONJA: Hiemke's was terrible last night. The regulars
toasting each other. Smashing their beermugs together so
hard, by the time they'd finished every pot in the place
was broken.

MARK: What's that blood on your blouse?

SONJA: Punter bit my breast didn't he.

MARK: Your nipple's still hard...

SONJA: It is when you touch me – Mark... Oh, those hands
know what they're doing...

MARK: I'm going to be a doctor one day... A general
practitioner. With a beard.

SONJA: You were examining that girl from the German
League[3] last night, the landlady said.

MARK: Juices are building up!

SONJA: Is that what Rosenberg[4] says? And Streicher[5]?

MARK: It's got to happen.

SONJA: Love is what's got to happen! You're too young.
You should wait a while.

MARK: Sonja – I'm sixteen years old! And I haven't made
love to that girl from the German League.

SONJA: I think...

MARK: Sonja: – last night I had to go and wash her smell
off my hands in the stream... I had to run away from the
dance and throw up! It was that pea soup...

SONJA: There's got to be love.

MARK: When is it love?

SONJA: For me it was Hardy. He worked at Tietz, as a
salesman. Mother waved her bony fist under my nose:
don't you dare do it before the wedding night! We went
and did it anyway. In the hut where he lived between the
main road and the railway. There were wax stencils lying
by the stove and political leaflets... He was sweet. I
loved it in his bed. Then suddenly there were hard
voices and loud footsteps in the garden. It was the SA[6] –
he told me to shush and let me out the window... I hid
in the bushes. I saw them beat him. They stuffed leaflets
into his mouth and dragged him out of the hut. A sick
laugh came out of my mouth: it was mother, she'd gone
and sent the SA after me because of the scandal!

MARK: God – Sonja!

JAKOB: Excuse me... Sonja – I left your milk under the step.

SONJA: A new May – a new milkman.

JAKOB: Dad slept in, so I did his round for him.

MARK: Sonja – Who's that?

SONJA: Don't you know Jakob?

PETER HUNDT: (*Who has joined them unobtrusively.*) You remember Jakob?

MARK: We're the same height...

JAKOB: You're a bit taller...

Scene 2

School toilets.

PETER HUNDT: (*Sings.*) I got drunk as a skunk,
    drunk as a skunk,
    drunk as a skunk with you
    last night.

MARK: I'm so excited! There's just so much to get excited about. This is such a perfect time to be young.

PETER HUNDT: D'you want a smoke?

MARK: Peter! Stealing from the doctor again! Black market cigarettes!

PETER HUNDT: Father's not bothered.

MARK: Do his patients like him poking around their insides with his hands smelling of tobacco?

PETER HUNDT: None of his patients ever notice.

MARK: A smoke?

PETER HUNDT: Go on then.
    (*They sing*)
    We got drunk as a skunk,
    drunk as a skunk,
    drunk as a skunk me and you
    last night...

PIMPF: Let me have a drag...

MARK: If you stick your head in the bog we'll let you have a drag then...

PETER HUNDT: Markus!

MARK: Haven't you heard – A German boy does not smoke! There you go, have a drag on that...

PIMPF: They're going to look up to me too now, 'cos they all look up to you. (*Exit.*)

MARK: Those little terrors worship us.

PETER HUNDT: They worship you. I'm just Peter Hundt.

MARK: I've been getting carried away a lot recently. There's a Swedish voice on the radio...it's so, so low. Father loves mother. He carried her over the threshold into our house. We were messing about recently and he tried to get me up the steps too, but we men.. we could only manage about one step between us. It was hysterical!

PETER HUNDT: In our house...ah you know...the piano's all dusty. And the leather strap for punishing me's been forgotten on top of a cupboard...

MARK: What's the matter with that doctor of yours... I remember once he got so angry 'cos you got a bad mark in German history the duelling scar on his forehead went bright red...

PETER HUNDT: He's been given a new job after all now – in Potsdam – in the big hospital.

MARK: Great.

PETER HUNDT: He's got a guilty conscience. He only got it because the hospital's been aryanised. Father says Ehrlicher was a good man.

MARK: This is the time of destiny – for German men to be be promoted and take responsibility. Foreigners can't hang on to all the best jobs!

PETER HUNDT: But Ehrlicher was good... Martin came home from Freiberg on Sunday night. Pale and withdrawn, like a ghost. Mother was shocked.

MARK: He always was a joker.

PETER HUNDT: He wants to get out of the mining college. Ideology's not going to make the ore any richer- he says – and Freiberg cathedral's no longer any comfort to him.

MARK: Yeah, so?

PETER HUNDT: Want another smoke?

MARK: Your brother's pathetic! He's letting the side down! We're all in this together, aren't we!

PETER HUNDT: I'm just Peter Hundt!

MARK: You're aryan!

PETER HUNDT: Come on, let's go back to the lesson!

MARK: The Führer says we're to show that teaching rabble no mercy!

PETER HUNDT: And no-one who's small and dark-haired should ever be allowed to forget they're small and dark-haired...

MARK: Come on, Peter! Us two'll always stick together. In Leipzig...now that's a city...you'll see...

PETER HUNDT: Once we've brought the alma mater to its knees...

MARK: We'll study medicine.

PETER HUNDT: We'll share a room.

MARK: That'll be the life!

Scene 3

Goetheplatz.

JAKOB: Hello, Peter!

PETER HUNDT: Jakob, old chap! What are you up to?

JAKOB: It's the third week of mourning so they let us off school.

PETER HUNDT: What school are you going to now?

JAKOB: In Caputh. There's a Jewish home we stay at during the week. They've got an emergency class for us lucky ones who've been chucked out of the German schools.

PETER HUNDT: What's it like? Is it bearable?

JAKOB: Just about. They bought thirty-six rabbits, four each for us to look after. We call the teachers by their first names, we've cleared the garden. I've spent a lot of time outdoors recently.

PETER HUNDT: No-one could get you out of the house before. If our mothers tried to make us play in the fresh air we'd hide under the table.

JAKOB: And play chemist's shops, that was the best.

PETER HUNDT: Remember we used to spend hours selling each other cremes and ointments.

JAKOB: God knows who started it all...

PETER HUNDT: You know – it was Bimbo, the monkey...

JAKOB: Oh of course, Bimbo...

PETER HUNDT: It was great.

JAKOB: How's Warweser?

PETER HUNDT: Warweser?

JAKOB: Aren't you best friends?

PETER HUNDT: Warweser and me – we're like Hagen and Eckart! Like the old Niebelungen...

JAKOB: Bye, Peter! (*Exit.*)

PETER HUNDT: See you!

KRISTA: Jewish scum like him defiles German society!

PETER HUNDT: Yes, Krista.

KRISTA: You needn't spit on him this time, Peter, I can still hear the May song they played at the German Girls' League afternoon...

PETER HUNDT: Yes, Krista.

KRISTA: Warweser's going out with me!

PETER HUNDT: Warweser's got taste!

KRISTA: How do I look, Peter?

PETER HUNDT: Like Diana, the Hunting Goddess.

KRISTA: Oh?

PETER HUNDT: Like Emmi Sonnemann[7].

KRISTA: Have you got a girlfriend? D'you want me to help you? The youngest Grohmann girl's got strange taste: she really fancies you. I've got that on very good authority.

PETER HUNDT: The youngest one? Er...

KRISTA: Not interested?

PETER HUNDT: We-ll!

KRISTA: You too, Peter Hundt, you're going to have to go the right way, just like all the rest of us, but we're in good hands. Last night I dreamed I was walking along a big, fat, soft finger... like the rubber truncheon my father wears on his belt – it was the Führer's finger. Peter, do you know how to kiss yet?

PETER HUNDT: I've got to go, Krista! Homework…

KRISTA: I do. Mark does. But he hasn't… You kiss me!

Scene 4

Little Ones

The Warwesers' house. VIOLA is posing half-naked while WILLO looks at her through his camera.

VIOLA: And the butter coupons had ended up in the living room again!

WILLO: Wasn't me.

VIOLA: Well it wasn't me!

WILLO: Look kitsch darling! Frail and lovelorn, less predatory! – and do stop thinking about that Viennese clown!

VIOLA: Bloody Schicklgruber[x] – and you're going to throw that radio out!

WILLO: On this sofa you're free. Now a bit freer – please!

VIOLA: Did you hear that? Was that Mark?

WILLO: He was nursed on those tits! Keep still, Vio.

VIOLA: Since he reached puberty, he's gone all shy…
When did I last see my great big son in all his glory? I don't even know if his pubic hair's thin or bushy.

WILLO: Kitscher!

VIOLA: And everything's so expensive! Twelve Reichsmarks the Hitler Youth uniform costs in his size!

WILLO: I'll get twelve Reichsmarks for one of these innocent pics.

VIOLA: Will you really?

WILLO: You bet. I meet the bloke at the Zoo Station and slip them inside his coat. He pays on the spot and pays well. In the old days it was Communist leaflets he used to carry round in his pants, now it's pictures like these. He's a good seller.

VIOLA: And I'm supposed to look kitsch… am I?
Communists?! What are you getting yourself into?!

WILLO: Your breasts are so round.

VIOLA: Missed my period again. I'm going to Ehrlichers' tomorrow.

WILLO: Go to Doctor Hundt.

VIOLA: Doctor Hundt's an animal!

WILLO: Where do you go to meet the angelmakers these days?

VIOLA: That's what Ehrlicher'll tell me. Not Doctor Hundt!

WILLO: Do you really want to bring another defenceless child into a world full of these bloodhounds?

VIOLA: It might be a girl...

WILLO: You want to keep it?

VIOLA: I've half made up my mind.

WILLO: And I'm supposed to jump for joy, am I?

VIOLA: Say it – what are you thinking...

MARK: Where's father's jacket?

VIOLA: Hanging on the bedroom door!

MARK: Could I help myself to a couple of Marks?

WILLO: Take a nice fat tenner, my boy!

Scene 5

Mark Buys Cheese

In the GLÜCKSLEBENS' grocer's shop.

REBEKKA: Can I help you?

MARK: Have you got any Roquefort?

REBEKKA: Roquefort? You're not quite with it, are you sir! These days I'm glad of that piece of Allgau. Shall I cut you some?

MARK: Is the son of the house in?

REBEKKA: Stay where you are!

MARK: What did I say that was so awful? Is your son in?

REBEKKA: Do you want some cheese or not?

MARK: Don't you let people see him?

REBEKKA: Don't buy anything. Please don't be offended, just go!

JAKOB: What do you want, Warweser?

REBEKKA: Jakob, don't come in!

MARK: Some cheese, damn it, did I say anything else?!

JAKOB: You go, mother.

REBEKKA: I need you to open that barrel of sauerkraut!

JAKOB: Am I your slave?!

REBEKKA: Yes you are, and don't answer back!

JAKOB: In my new class I'm two heads taller than the other children, I sit there, on my own, so tall my knees stick up over the table...with the toy train just going round and round in circles... I'm not a moron! Do you realise, Mother! Sometimes I still want to exchange a few words with people like me...

REBEKKA: People like you?

JAKOB: No need to be like that.

REBEKKA: Where's father?

JAKOB: Gone out!

REBEKKA: Give me the chisel, you ought to be ashamed making me do it by myself! (*Exit.*

JAKOB slices cheese with a large knife.)

MARK: I went to Berlin once, when the Führer spoke at the Reich's sport field. He doesn't really like speaking in Berlin. I want to go to the next party rally in Nuremberg with all the comrades... The words echoed so much, falling on the frozen square, there were tiny little pieces of ice raining down out of an empty sky. It was a sharp, frosty January evening, the Führer spoke, and the sky was heavenly blue... And everything around us suddenly turned cold, very cold.

JAKOB: Tell me when to stop.

MARK: Don't cut so fast. When I was little I had a brown terrier with a bent white ear. Until a travelling circus stopped on the hill and my dog got a sniff of their shaggy old bear. Then he ran away... Stop!

JAKOB: (*Weighs the cheese and works out the price on some packing paper.*) Six fifty.

MARK: That's terrible. My mother spends that much on food for a whole week.

JAKOB: The Allgau's good value for money.

(*MARK gives him a ten mark note.*)

JAKOB: (*Counts out money.*) Seven – Nine fifty – Nine ninety – Nine ninety-five– Nine ninety-six – Ninety-seven – Ninety-eight. Ten.

MARK: Right.

JAKOB: Thank you.

MARK: Yeah, I want to get another dog... but will he stay with me? And not run away again? What'll happen if he smells a shaggy old bear?

Scene 6

Evening Phone Call

WILLO: Warweser.

PETER HUNDT: Hundt. Evening, Mr. Warweser. How are you?

WILLO: I'm trying to cut down on my smoking.

PETER HUNDT: You put me to shame. I'm already on my third packet today.

VIOLA: (*Shouting between them.*) That's unhealthy!

WILLO: That was Viola, plucking the cigarette from my lips. So, Hundt, is that the small talk taken care of?

PETER HUNDT: Yes.

WILLO: And now you want me to call Mark out of his bedroom?

PETER HUNDT: If it's not too much bother...

WILLO: (*Shouting.*) Mark!

MARK: Hi, Peter...

PETER HUNDT: It's Krista... You've driven her wild!

MARK: Aren't I the stud?!

PETER HUNDT: You are! Seems I am too.

MARK: I'm really tired. I was just getting undressed.

PETER HUNDT: My God! Haven't you got any clothes on?

MARK: My father threw me his red silk dressing gown.

PETER HUNDT: That's disgusting.

MARK: Feels gorgeous.

PETER HUNDT: Get off your dirty bastard!

MARK: What?

PETER HUNDT: There's a moth buzzing about round my head. A big yellow one, colour of butter.

MARK: Well swat it then! I'm tired. Good night. (*Hangs up.*)

PETER HUNDT: Night. (*Hangs up.*) Night. In the Goetheplatz a dog catches its own tail.

Scene 7

Grass Wet With Dew

Early morning in front of the WARWESERS' house.

JAKOB: I got up early. I delivered all the milk. Mother'll be amazed.

MARK: I got up early specially. Now I'm shivering here on this garden chair.

JAKOB: You look tired...

MARK: But I'm seeing you...

JAKOB: Do you want me to stay?

MARK: Alright!

JAKOB: Alright.

MARK: Sit down!

JAKOB: Alright. (*Kneels on the grass.*)
(*MARK gets off his chair and also kneels in the grass.*)
Now we've both got wet trousers.

WILLO: Keep smiling just like that! (*Photographs Jakob with his Leica.*)

MARK: That's my father! Always making a fool of himself in front of my friends. He's not one of your UFA[9] starlets!

WILLO: He's the wrong race for that, which makes him very attractive as far as I'm concerned.

MARK: Father!

WILLO: You can recite the distinguishing features of the nordic race by heart. You've recited the distinguishing features of the nordic race so often, now I know them off by heart: Stature: tall; skull: long, narrow; face: long, narrow; forehead: narrow, inclined back; nose: long, slender; chin: slender, pointed; genitals: thin, lips:

thin...skin: white. Everything's long and thin with the good guys, eh? A narrow skull's only got room for a narrow brain.

MARK: Father!

WILLO: Are you going to give all that stuff up now, Mark?

JAKOB: I've got to go.

WILLO: Me too. Fire up the old Steyr

MARK: Are you going to print his picture?

WILLO: When I get back from Berlin. It would be nice if you could come with me, lads, but you've got to go to school haven't you... Rats! Cheerio. (*Exit.*)

MARK: Sorry about him!

JAKOB: Your father's a social creature.

MARK: He's a party animal with no parties to go to... I'm not like him... I need my old friends, and occasionally I need a new friend...

JAKOB: Everything's so shut in. You're stuck at home with the family too, do you find yourself treading an ever narrower path too? Yesterday I could have done with a very different kind of friend yesterday...

MARK: Only yesterday? Not today? Not every day?

JAKOB: You're being very friendly, Warweser.

MARK: Let's be friends then! Let's kill off the boys inside us... I want to meet you in the evening, I want you to be my first friend as a man!

JAKOB: You intrigue me. A little. Do you ever go to the old cemetery?

MARK: We can go there tonight.

JAKOB: But it's got to be late.

MARK: The old cemetery's next to Hiemke's biergarten, where the diehards go and sit out under paper lanterns.

JAKOB: I want to get some pleasure out of my fear. And one night I want to go where the diehards go and sit out under their paper lanterns. Will you pick me up from the shop?

MARK: Just before ten?

JAKOB: The night will be the Arab cloth that hides my Jewish nose.

MARK: In a moment my mother'll be asking why her son's not in the kitchen drinking his morning coffee. In a moment the children will be here on their way to school...

JAKOB: Time for me to go, Warweser! So...

MARK: Jakob, you're so beautiful it hurts.

JAKOB: Warweser says that to me?! I'm grinning... (*Exit.*)

MARK: God, my cheeks...red with shame.

Scene 8

Round This Place

MARK: You'll come to heel and lie down, you're my girlfriend!

KRISTA: Yes, Mark..

MARK: I don't need to keep you on a tight leash to prove that I'm close to you!

KRISTA: There's a gang of us going to the flicks later. You and me?

MARK: I don't watch love films.

KRISTA: You can learn about love from love films! You and me?

MARK: No, Krista, I can't... Our company's on guard at the Schlageter memorial and there's a meeting tonight.

PIMPF: (*Babbles mockingly.*)
I'm the biggest pig
round this place
'cos I consort
with the Jewish race.

MARK: (*Shouting.*) D'you want me to knock your head off, you little piece of shit?! – Heil Hitler, Jungsturmmann!

MAN WITH SQUINT: Heil Hitler!

KRISTA: Heil Hitler!

MARK: Heil Hitler, mother!

VIOLA: Mark, are you trying to make me sick all over again?!

MARK: We're going to form the guard at the Schlageter[10] memorial...

VIOLA: I want you out of those boots, it's turned out warm this afternoon – let's go to Schöder's – they've got ice cream today…

MARK: I'm going to Schöder's with these boots on – it'll be full today, they've got lemon…

VIOLA: Lemon and boot oil: just what I fancy.

MARK: And strawberry. And raspberry.

VIOLA: And lemon.

MARK: Pink May. Eighteen degrees in the shade.

VIOLA: Yellow May. Thirty-five degrees in the sun.

MARK: Shall I offer you my arm?

VIOLA: You've grown again! Do you really want to wear those boots…

MARK: Mother – I have to!

VIOLA: Hello, Miss Schmidt!

MARK: Heil Hitler, Comrade Teacher!

VIOLA: Afternoon, Mrs Glücksleben. Has she lost her tongue?!

PIMPF: (*Babbles mockingly.*)
I'm the biggest pig
round this place
'cos I consort
with the Jewish race.

Scene 9

Kiss Me

Old Cemetery. Beside Petra von Paschke's grave.

JAKOB: I just need a quick slash.

MARK: Do you have to go pissing all over poor Petra's brain?

JAKOB: Ha, ha, Warweser! Blast, I've fallen in!

MARK: You want to lie down and try it out?

JAKOB: Here, eat some!

MARK: You swine!

JAKOB: Look out! You'll bump into that angel.

MARK: Aah!

JAKOB: Are you afraid of angels?

MARK: Yes... I'm afraid of angels.

JAKOB: They're singing over at Hiemke's. Nationalist
songs.

MARK: Horst Wessel Song[11]. 'Rome awake, the sky is
Prussian blue'.

JAKOB: Let's go home, Warweser!

MARK: Already?

JAKOB: I'm knackered! Twenty crates we had to unload
from the cart this lunchtime, father and me, and the
gelding's like a magnet for midges... I'm cold!

MARK: You were working this afternoon...

JAKOB: No I spent the time playing with my prick!

MARK: The things you say.

JAKOB: You're not like the boys at boarding school. I used
to go to a boarding school in the forest. It was very
progressive. Only the Jewish Union had to withdraw my
scholarship. That school made me. It taught me I'm a
perfectly functioning human machine! Why didn't you
go there? You could have gone. We would have been
together. Karl, my first friend, he's in Holland now. They
have Charlie Chaplin films in the cinemas there, Rin-tin-
tin films... He sees them all...

MARK: Who's Rin-tin-tin?

JAKOB: Rin-tin-tin's a dog.

MARK: Jakob, the beautiful! Jakob, the worldly! Jakob, the
best boy in the whole world!

JAKOB: The Jungsturmmann with the squint's just come
out of Hiemke's. He's doing up his buckle. Whistling,
getting ready to leave. Is he going to come this way?

MARK: He's on duty. Hitler Youth patrol. He'll make sure
none of the comrades has fallen into a grave drunk. He'll
clean up the sick in the Goetheplatz. He'll keep a look
out for illegal associations.

JAKOB: Aren't we an illegal association, Warweser?

MARK: Let's go home!

JAKOB: Let's go home!

(*They stand motionless before one another, staring in each
other's faces.*)

MARK: What is it about us, Jakob.

JAKOB: Ask Magnus Hirschfeld[12], father to both of us.

MARK: Who?

JAKOB: Magnus Hirschfeld.

MARK: Why's he our father?

JAKOB: Don't you know anything! Anything! Have you at least heard of Onan in the Bible?

MARK: I'm not too good on the Bible.

JAKOB: Onan spilt his seed on the ground. For that he had to die.

MARK: I do that sometimes.

JAKOB: I don't. A religious Jew's not allowed to waste his seed.

MARK: Are you religious?

JAKOB: No, I sleep in the same room as my parents.

MARK: Go home, then...

JAKOB: Are we still okay, Warweser?

MARK: Why do you keep on using my surname? Call me 'Mark'. 'Mark'!

JAKOB: I don't want to..

MARK: Kiss me!

(*Kiss on the mouth.*)

JAKOB: Could you feel my tongue?

MARK: I want to feel it deeper inside my throat. More please!

(*Kiss on the mouth.*)

JAKOB: Enough, that's enough! There, swallow it! I want your tongue in my throat!

(*Kiss on the mouth.*)

MARK: Satisfied?

JAKOB: Confused. (*Walks away hurriedly.*)

MARK: Red with shame. (*Leaves.*)

SONJA: Heil, Mark...

MARK: Sonja...

SONJA: Mark?! Mark – what is it?!

MARK: Sonja – I'm in love.

SONJA: I was in love too...

MARK: With Hardy.

SONJA: Poor thing, your forehead's all wet... My Hardy
had blood all down his neck when he came back from
Kegelheim, from the torture chamber, and when we were
married, my bridegroom had a black eye and my mouth
was still swollen when we said 'I do'... I too was a bride
once... It's so beautiful when you say 'Hardy'...

MARK: Hardy.

SONJA: Hardy.

MARK: Hardy.

Scene 10

A Good Morning in the Marriage Bed

WILLO: Vio – pale, little nightingale... Did we have to lose
all our friends? Did they all have to go into exile? After
'33 it was a relief at first to be too pale to be persecuted.
One pale face amongst all the others – I fit in with the
Third Reich – how I long to see dark skin.

VIOLA: Is my husband going to make Sunday breakfast?

WILLO: Sleep well?

VIOLA: Hm.

WILLO: Hm.

VIOLA: Three plates, because there are three of us...and a
little empty plate for Anna.

WILLO: We're going to have to tell Mark – you're four
months gone.

VIOLA: It's a bit embarrassing.

MARK: It's as crowded as the Anhalter Station in here, with
everyone trying to leave for the country – smells like the
Ahlbeck train too.

VIOLA: Hello, is your back sore?

WILLO: Well, you made yourself at home, didn't you! I
don't know what's got into you, Mark, sneaking into
mummy and daddy's bed in the middle of the night!
Sixteen years old!

VIOLA: Leave him alone, Willo, it was sweet of him. He
put his big warm hand round my cold foot. It was just

like the old days, when he slept with us as a little boy, then he'd always lie the other way round.

WILLO: Like this.

VIOLA: Mark – do you like babies?

MARK: I don't know.

VIOLA: Do you want to have children?

MARK: Me?

VIOLA: You don't want any children?

MARK: I don't know.

VIOLA: Don't you like children?

MARK: I'm never going to have any.

VIOLA: Won't you be good to our Anna?

MARK: What Anna?

VIOLA: Who's in my tummy. – The one in my tummy: it's going to be a girl and she's going to be called Anna!

WILLO: And I made her.

MARK: Oh, right.

Scene 11

White Sheets

PETER HUNDT: D'you want a smoke...

MARK: D'you want a smoke...

PETER HUNDT: My father dropped a full packet in the hall this morning when he went off to help Uncle Hans with the slaughter, he did it on purpose to apologise for hitting me yesterday after church... (*Smoothes his hair back.*) A red welt.

MARK: Your dad's getting heavy-handed in his old age.

PETER HUNDT: If you wet a cloth you can use it like a cane... It doesn't half sting! Father grabbed my tracksuit top, it was soaking in the tub, and the zip...

MARK: Oooh!

(*Enter KRISTA.*)

PETER HUNDT: Don't stand on my sheets, the June sun's bleaching them clean!

KRISTA: Put your cigs out! My brother's coming.

PETER HUNDT: The reason I smoke so much is because the Hitler Youth doesn't allow it.

KRISTA: Does Warweser smoke too?!

MARK: Can't you see...

PETER HUNDT: He's not one of your little Baldur[13] boys.

KRISTA: My brother's polished his boots, now he's putting on his white gloves... And at teatime he'll tell horror stories about the Catholic boy scouts... If it wasn't for that, I'd take you with me, Peter! Did you hear that, Mark?

PETER HUNDT: Well I'm a Catholic. And this afternoon I want to be up a tree with my air rifle shooting birds. Birds and girls!

KRISTA: Peter's always such a laugh... Isn't he Mark?

MARK: The German Girls' League makes such a mess of the women! – Let your hair down. Wear something red!

KRISTA: But I haven't got...

(*JAKOB enters.*)

PETER HUNDT: Hey Jakob – old chap! Come and sit down!

JAKOB: Yes – Peter's a good soul... You're – a weak woman. And I won't have to fight Warweser either...

KRISTA: How dare you – Jew?!

MARK: What is it?

JAKOB: Does there have to be something, brownshirt? Does there?

(*Silence.*)

JAKOB: Can you see the cemetery from here?

MARK: Can you see the cemetery from here?

JAKOB: And Petra von Paschke whispering and sighing under her thin blanket of earth...

MARK: Petra von Paschke's our angel...

JAKOB: It was nice...

MARK: You feel ok about yesterday?

(*Silence.*)

Tonight let's go to the Paradise Cinema.

JAKOB: Give me a whistle – in our back yard. Just don't kick the metal bucket against the door of the stall when

you're creeping about. The gelding'll start neighing, and once he's started he'll never stop! I'm going to have to hide from danger like a chicken in a thunder storm...
(*Hurries off away from PIMPF and the YOUNG MAN WITH THE SQUINT, who enter from behind.*)
KRISTA: That wasn't funny, Mark! Not funny at all...
(*Walks to PIMPF and the YOUNG MAN WITH THE SQUINT.*)

PETER HUNDT: Your round, carp-like mouth seems to have got even rounder and more carp-like recently...

MARK: The cherries are turning ripe and red.

PETER HUNDT: Not just the cherries...

MARK: It's this wind. Cooling my thick-skinned face. Hey, Peter...

PETER HUNDT: So I'm a good soul, am I? A good soul?!

PART TWO

Scene 1

Mourning Eggs

In the GLÜCKSLEBENS' kitchen.

REBEKKA: Did Joseph Süss collect you from school?

JAKOB: In that stupid horse and cart!

REBEKKA: They took away his motor car.

JAKOB: We're too big for it now anyway, the five of us wouldn't all fit in the back of the Mercedes.

REBEKKA: We always had a nice time. Those afternoon rides to Petzwow Castle.

JAKOB: I can remember us all standing on the running board to have our photograph taken: Cohn, Sieghard Voss, Regine and little Marian.

REBEKKA: You can peel the eggs.

JAKOB: I washed my hands with carbolic.

REBEKKA: Good boy.

JAKOB: Mummy...

REBEKKA: I'm making Se'udat Hawra. It's for people in mourning. Just bread and a few boiled eggs. No more. It's easy to prepare.

JAKOB: Why are we having Se'udat Hawra today?

REBEKKA: We're just having Se'udat Hawra. Because it's cheap. And because the eggs in the shop won't be fresh tomorrow.

JAKOB: Can I have an egg now?

REBEKKA: We don't eat between meals in this house!

JAKOB: I'm hungry.

REBEKKA: Very well.

JAKOB: Please may I have some salt?

REBEKKA: No!

JAKOB: Please.

REBEKKA: No! It's unhealthy! You shouldn't eat salt at your age. Do you want to get a face full of spots?

JAKOB SNR: (*Enters.*) Right.

REBEKKA: So Dad – d'you shut up shop?

JAKOB SNR: Can I have an egg now?

REBEKKA: The two of you are impossible!

JAKOB SNR: Pass the salt, lad!

JAKOB: There you are, Dad.

REBEKKA: Where's the egg slicer?

JAKOB SNR: Here's the egg slicer. You can play a tune on
it: Zssing... I'm exhausted today, it all seems hopeless.

JAKOB: I met Mark Warweser twice, and...

REBEKKA: Your walks with young Master Warweser have
got to stop. The first one you kept secret. Yesterday I
almost died with worry.

JAKOB: This is terrible!

JAKOB SNR: This is Se'udat Hawra – a meal to strengthen
those in mourning. The mourner doesn't sit in his usual
chair, but on a low stool. He takes his shoes off and puts
on slippers made of cloth or felt. He sits and mourns...

REBEKKA: Stop jabbering, Dad! Out with it, Jakob!

JAKOB: What's between Mark Warweser and me isn't
friendship. It's biology.

REBEKKA: What's that mean?!

JAKOB: His body tells me something only I understand
and my body tells him something only he understands.

JAKOB SNR: Aha.

JAKOB: We kissed with our tongues... the way lovers
kiss...not brothers!

REBEKKA: I knew something like this would happen. I
knew it would! That terrible town's got hold of you! –
And stop scraping that spoon with your finger nails!

JAKOB SNR: It's just a bit of old dough stuck to a spoon.
That's all.

REBEKKA: If only we'd been kept apart. In the stetl this
wouldn't have happened. A German boy would never
have grabbed you, thrown you on the ground – I wish
they'd hurt you rather than seduced you – 'Brothers'
indeed.

JAKOB SNR: Quiet, Rebekka!

REBEKKA: And take the milk sieve off your face! Get it away from your flesh – now you've spoiled that sieve!

JAKOB SNR: Get a grip on yourself, Rebekka! Have you lost your mind?!

REBEKKA: Dad, go and pray with him!

JAKOB: Yeah, dad, come and pray with me!

JAKOB SNR: Have I got two women in the house now then?

REBEKKA: Not on your life!

JAKOB SNR: Take a good look at him, Rebekka Glücksleben, born Rebekka Brillenschleifer! Between the two of us we couldn't manage a Haarlem blacksmith. A frail little Berlin beauty's the best we could do... Aren't I right, lad, aren't I right?

REBEKKA: And you laugh about it!

JAKOB SNR: Well, what am I supposed to do, cry?! And you, do you want to stand under a chuppa with a woman, like your father and mother? You don't? – Well, listen to your heart! But try to feel the Jew inside you, think of Jerusalem, before you go creeping into his bed like a concubine lying down to die. Look in the mirror and think of David, be proud, Jewish boys don't cry – your Dad says so!

REBEKKA: Why us!

JAKOB SNR: We can handle this, Rebekka! – And you're going to bring your young man here for supper, next Friday, when we have guests! And there'll be dumplings to eat and lumps in our throats.

Scene 2

Humid Night With Distant Thunder

In PETER HUNDT's room, a glass ashtray and a skull, Fritz, lying close together.

MARK: I'm sweating like Attila the Hun.

PETER HUNDT: Go to sleep.

MARK: That food was too rich.

PETER HUNDT: The boiled pork was disgusting!

MARK: I'm too full. (*Lays his hand on PETER's chest.*)

PETER HUNDT: Attila, get your paw off my ribs and stop trying to paint pictures in my sweat!

MARK: Jakob let me put my hand in his shirt when we kissed yesterday, he held it from the outside through the cloth, let my finger play with his left nipple without saying a word...

PETER HUNDT: Oh – God help us...

MARK: Gone are the snow white lambs of childhood...

PETER HUNDT: Jakob?! Not Krista?!

MARK: Jakob! Jakob from the Jewish shop... If he were here he wouldn't leave the room a virgin.
Yesterday...racing to the cemetery, without either of us saying anything, we both crawled deep into the bushes. And there we kissed. I swallowed his spit like a ball of foam. A dead nightingale lay on the gravel path, it was red, already half decomposed...

PETER HUNDT: Oh Mother, oh God... That's a shock!
(*Jumps up as if stung by a tarantula, then kneels on the floor.*) That cool, calm Jewish boy. He sent me postcards from boarding school, postcards of black castles against white skies. Has his soul been struck by a thunderbolt from the rain of steel? Crawling round in the bushes kissing a – homo?

MARK: Have you started praying for me?!

PETER HUNDT: I'm afraid of kneeling down to pray in case it gets you going, God in Heaven – poor Jakob!

MARK: Jakob's like me!

PETER HUNDT: It's awful the way you treat Jakob, the Jew! Is it a crime to be born a Jew, do I have to remind you about the race laws? How do you think Jakob feels about decrees that make him different from us, can't you see them failing with that pathetic shop? I can see, Warweser, that the majority of people in this country no longer want the Nuremberg Laws[11] enforced, but no-one's asking the majority any more, Warweser, and no-one's ever going to ask us because we were still kids when the brown fart spread everywhere, but you go and spit in a Jew's face without even thinking!

MARK: (*Shouts.*) I kiss Jews!

PETER HUNDT: (*Shouts.*) You bastard!

(*Long silence.*)

MARK: Have a smoke!

PETER HUNDT: I'm scared to reach for the packet, if I so much as move you might grab hold of me again.

(*Long silence.*)

PETER HUNDT: It's just hormones, Warweser – hormones...

MARK: Hormones?

PETER HUNDT: Yes, your hormones are going mad. Haven't you noticed?

MARK: All I notice is my heart beating.

PETER HUNDT: You poor sod.

(*From outside the flickering light, rumble and crash of a storm.*)

SONJA: (*Hurrying outside, trying to cover herself from the rain with her hands.*) God, the seam of my dress is running... (*Exit.*)

Scene 3

Swastika on Blue Sky

Early morning, in front of Warweser's house.

KRISTA: What are you taking the flag to school for? You shouldn't be carrying the flag of the German Reich rolled up!

MARK: I was the athletics champion. And the champion always gets the flag as a prize. In the last few weeks I've not done so well. Now I've got to take the flag back.

KRISTA: You're not exactly treating it like your pride and joy.

MARK: I won't contradict a beautiful woman.

KRISTA: Thank you for the coffee and strawberry cake at the baker's yesterday.

MARK: Schöder's is cheap. Standing. It's nothing.

KRISTA: I liked standing there with you.

MARK: You dragged me along.

KRISTA: Did you regret it?

MARK: No, not at all! It felt very different with you, we go well together so well, like a pair from the same set... And everyone can see it...

KRISTA: A girl from the League says you've been with a prostitute...

MARK: What a cow!

KRISTA: So you've not been doing well at athletics?

MARK: So what?

KRISTA: So what? So what? You're descending into the poxy Jew-infested gutter of love! Well not with me! You've forgotten the Führer in all your spring awakening and you shouldn't be carrying the flag of the German Reich rolled up!

MARK: Krista, where are you going!

KRISTA: I have to say good morning to my League leader's fiancée

REBEKKA: (*With the milk.*) It's just Jakob's mother, young master Warweser!

MARK: Good morning, Mrs Glücksleben.

REBEKKA: My husband and I don't want Jakob hanging round with those big boys on the corner.

MARK: We're not going to the corner! We want to go into Berlin, to the cinema.

REBEKKA: The cinema?! Will you get back in one piece before the curfew? Does that swastika make you as strong as Max Schmeling[15]?

MARK: I've got strong arms, me.

REBEKKA: You're flabby. Your mother buys a lot of potatoes. You should grow your own. Then you could afford good white fish from our shop. But the Warwesers plant fir trees and an English lawn! If I had you under my wing the first thing I'd do is put a stop to the Warwesers buying potatoes. My husband's got a bad back this morning. Otherwise he'd have come himself. He

asked me to give you a message, but I've forgotten what
it was.

MARK: Oh?

REBEKKA: I'm sure it wasn't important.

MARK: Might have been.

REBEKKA: Goodness me – what was it?

MARK: You're having me on!

REBEKKA: You've got real bedroom eyes! You try to make
a joke but it turns out sensual – strange, strange… My
Jakob keeps admiring his flat stomach in the mirror
when he thinks I'm not looking… I always wanted a
girl… And this is my punishment for putting ribbons in
his hair when he was a child. On Friday he'll be waiting
for you in the kitchen wearing a white frock coat,
whether he likes it or not. You're invited to a Jewish
supper, eight o'clock in the evening, I expect you to be
on time!

MARK: This Friday!

REBEKKA: We could say next week… the week after…

MARK: What did your husband say?

REBEKKA: Is there any food you don't like?

MARK: I eat everything.

REBEKKA: Then is there anything special you would like?

MARK: I eat everything.

REBEKKA: Well then, blanched vegetables and peppercorn
bread. It's food non-Orthodox Jews eat. That'll suit you.
Jakob will spit in the pan, he hates that food, but it
serves him right for all his canoodling. (*Exit.*)

Scene 4

Goetheplatz.

KRISTA: You're wearing Diviné Rossée make-up but you're
artificial, it suits you. You are wearing Diviné Rossée –
my Girl's League leader say you shouldn't wear make-
up, not when you're pregnant! Just this minute my
brother crossed your son's name off the list for the
leadership college at Bad Berka that starts tomorrow.
Mark's taken it very badly! On the radio the Reich's

meteorologist has forecast storms and rain.

VIOLA: Goose.

KRISTA: Those heels are far too high, Mrs Warweser!
You'll damage the unborn child in your womb!
Tomorrow, when the holidays start my brother's going to
take me to the Goethe Festival in Weimar. And then
further into Saxony for the summer, training young élite
SS[16] at Colditz Castle. I'll have Hitler's finest young
men for company.

VIOLA: You do know children can be conceived before
marriage, don't you?

KRISTA: We live in fertile times.

Scene 5

In the Rain Outside

*MARK's room: a washstand with jug and bowl, which can be concealed
behind a bright curtain: a bed built inside a cupboard.*

MARK: (*Enters with JAKOB.*) My room's more of a
cupboard. See what I mean.

JAKOB: Like a hotel.

MARK: I only come up here to sleep. My parents converted
the attic for me when I was twelve… I prefer to spend
my time downstairs. I need people around me, I need
life.

JAKOB: If I had my own room, it'd be more of a
sanctuary… I've never had a room of my own. At
boarding school, in Gutendorf, there were twenty of us to
a dormitory… (*Opens the doors of the cupboard bed.*)

MARK: It's very small…

JAKOB: I've got a fold-up bed in my parents' room.

MARK: Peter Hundt's got a box mattress on bricks. (*Folds
the bed down.*) Have a seat!

JAKOB: How was your report?

MARK: Good. And yours?

JAKOB: We don't get marks, we had a group discussion,
afterwards I was given *The Sorrows of Young Werther*[17] and
the little ones all got a game. I'm going away tomorrow.

MARK: You're going away?

JAKOB: It's the holidays, have you forgotten?

MARK: You're going away?

JAKOB: To Wettelbrunn in Baden, down in the South. The family are called Engel. They've got a daughter – Geli, she's thirteen. I stayed with them before, when I was a child. Now I'm going back as a man. I'm really looking forward to it... Mother wanted to me to go to Zurich, but it was impossible to arrange in the time. If I went to Zurich I'd never come back. That's the way it is, Warweser!

MARK: You're going away. For a holiday!

JAKOB: Yes – a holiday! – Is that your Bentley outside in the rain?

MARK: It's a Steyr – Shit, Father and Mother!
(*They lie in each others arms.*)

MARK: Is your hat on the back of the chair downstairs?

JAKOB: Will they come straight in here?

MARK: My jacket's on the back of the chair too.

JAKOB: Your hair's soaking.

MARK: Look – they'll be here in a minute.

JAKOB: And you've been going round all day with your flies done up the wrong way in forest green trousers at that... (*Buttons up MARK's trousers*)

MARK: And two of your four trouser buttons are undone...
(*Undoes two of JAKOB's trouser buttons. Each hurriedly feeling for the other's genitals.*)

JAKOB: Do you know what you want to be?

MARK: A doctor with a beard. And you?

JAKOB: (*Whispers*) A newspaper editor... in Palestine.
(*There's a knock at the door. JAKOB stands up, folds the bed up and closes the cupboard doors.*)
Mrs Warweser.

VIOLA: Hello. Call me Vio.

JAKOB: When's the baby coming?

VIOLA: November. Can you tell?

JAKOB: When Auntie Jopie went into labour, I sat in the room with her, we could hear the cars in the

Wesperstrasse while the little one came... But the man
who did the circumcision was very rough. I'm
uncircumcised, my parents didn't want it done to me at
the time. In Palestine I'll get myself circumcised straight
away, but in a hospital, under general anaesthetic!

VIOLA: You're emigrating? Everyone is, what a shame!
Though in Palestine there are palm trees and a red
moon. I wouldn't mind strolling under palm trees either.

JAKOB: Mother wrote and applied. Then they sent her
loads of forms. On the one hand staying's gradually
getting to be impossible, on the other you keep needing
more papers to be allowed to go! Bureaucracy is the
worst thing about this country since '33, my parents say,
now we're supposed to declare all our assets, bank
confidentiality's a joke.

VIOLA: Every morning I wake up happy that I'm having a
baby, then when I'm properly awake, I can feel a
tightening round my heart that could harm the child. I
want to get out of here too some times, I can tell you.
Home, I want to go home...but my sweet burden here...
My husband will do anything for me, but this... And his
German Nationalist family in Lübeck would never put
up with it, it would be as bad as him not joining the Nazi
party back then...then we'd no longer have their support
to fall back on every year... And how are we supposed
to live? I come from the village of Brook in Lübeck Bay.
But what am I supposed to do now in the village of
Brook in Lübeck Bay? There'll be a war soon. Running
away's the thing to do. Like the white horse... But I
won't get far on my own, I'm not clever enough! When I
was a girl, everyone kept on telling me I wasn't very
clever and sooner or later I believed them.

JAKOB: Does your husband, does he come from the coast
too?

VIOLA: Yes. Nordlichter. We both do.

JAKOB: Nordic. Strange, strange...

WILLO: (*Rushing past, shakes Jakob's hand.*)
A dream come true: holding the soft hand of my little

friend in my ink-stained paw.

VIOLA: An important visitor.

WILLO: I've developed your portrait – pocket size. I keep it under the cloth on my desk. Sometimes I look at it secretly – of course I'd rather enlarge it to fifty by forty and hang it in the living room. In the past I had mulatto, Chinese, African girls...

MARK: I'm confiscating that picture later!

WILLO: You never asked for it...

MARK: I've got the original...

VIOLA: That's the kettle... I'll lay the table for a nice family tea in the living room. (*Exit.*)

WILLO: I am/was – photographer to the stars. Used to do studio pictures. I had the equipment to do snapshots too. I specialised in first night parties and good nudes... Now if I hang around outside the film studios long enough they let me take pictures of the extras. I saw that Rökk woman[18] last week, she's got fat legs and dances like a cow. The black girls have all swum away across the water... Oh little Jakob, if this was 1919, I'd photograph you naked, it can be art, it is great art, and you look like the young Gertrud Kolmar[19]. And I'd sell the prints in a queer pub in Berlin, the 'Black Pig', may it rest in peace, in Berlin NW4... I'd make you a rich young man, with seven fur coats... D'you believe that?

JAKOB: No.

MARK: There are parts of my soul hardly know the word 'father'!

WILLO: And it's not 1919...

Scene 6

Through July and August

Light from MARK's window.

MAN IN OVERCOAT: Sshh, quiet! A light.

PETER HUNDT: It's only Warweser. He can't sleep. So he takes a detective novel up to bed with him. I know his routine.

MAN IN OVERCOAT: Then off you go, little Hundt! Just
be careful not to run into the wrong people... You
scared?

PETER HUNDT: It's my decision... I've had enough of
this Nazi crap...

MAN IN OVERCOAT: Right. Here's the leaflets. Hold on
to them. And be quick!

PETER HUNDT: (*Breathing rapidly, whispers*) Freedom for
Thälmann[20]...

MAN IN OVERCOAT: Be swift and silent, like a black
arrow... You're quick and nimble... You know where
you're going: Orenstein and Koppel – give the packet to
the night watchman, just leave it there. Wait, better make
sure first it really is Jupp in there. D'you know Jupp?

PETER HUNDT: I've seen him.

MAN IN OVERCOAT: Then off you go! Where's your
bike?

PETER HUNDT: There...

MAN IN OVERCOAT: Jupp'll phone through the code-
word once you're there... Till then my heart'll be
beating faster... You're still a boy! (*Both exit quickly in
different directions.*)

In MARK's room.

MAN WITH SQUINT: Too many men are strapping oaks
one day then floating black and swollen in the lake the
next. Write to Krista in Colditz!

MARK: And?

MAN WITH SQUINT: What?!

MARK: Heil Hitler, Jungsturmmann!

MAN WITH SQUINT: You're built like a tree... Where's
all your sap gone? Are you turning against us
completely?

MARK: You're drunk.

MAN WITH SQUINT: A German man...

MARK: Can hold his beer!

MAN WITH SQUINT: You're okay. Comradeship, Mark,

old comrades... Tomorrow we're taking a motor cycle to bits, the day after there are manoeuvres in the woods and Friday's our day on the shooting range at Treuenbrietzen. The Wessel song on their lips, the Comrades bake potatoes every evening, fires aglow on the hills...

MARK: An excellent programme of activities, comrade!

MAN WITH SQUINT: A wonderful summer.

Scene 7

At Table

In the GLÜCKSLEBENS' kitchen, a table with a white cloth, a pot on the stove.

REBEKKA: Do it whichever way you want, Jakob! There's the blanched vegetables... The peppercorn bread's already in the oven – I put the hartshorn infusion in yesterday... You'll need to reduce the vegetables with milk. Dad's bringing some wine up from the shop. Sh!
(*A loud knock at the door.*)

JAKOB SNR: (*Enters, puts two wine bottles on the table.*) Right. There's your Amselfelder for you!
(*Silence.*)

JAKOB SNR: (*Tasting what's in the pan.*) Hm, reminds me of your old domestic science teacher, Jakob. Old Miss Selig, the anaemic vegetarian...

JAKOB: I spat in the pan, dad...

JAKOB SNR: That's what it's like...

REBEKKA: Go and fetch the young man, Jakob Senior!

JAKOB SNR: My hat, Rebekka!

JAKOB: (*Passing the hat.*) Here, Dad...

JAKOB SNR: Why couldn't you stay with the Engels, near Switzerland, near the secret path across the border? Your friend's got a certificate of Aryanisation, you don't, if you fall in love, it'll be against the race laws. What if it hadn't been me at the door... what if it had been storm troopers? (*Exit.*)

REBEKKA: Mrs Warweser's huge already. Her stomach's

enormous.

JAKOB: It's coming in November.

REBEKKA: So soon? Soon the forests will go to sleep.

JAKOB: And the wild geese will all fly south...

REBEKKA: Footsteps on the stairs? – And look at you!
A strange young bride you make...

JAKOB: You were a young bride.

REBEKKA: Bathsheba, Susanna, me – and you...the same
thing...and the night always has the same three stars...

JAKOB SNR: (*Enters with MARK.*) Here. The photographer
seemed taken aback, his wife was asleep... They were
sitting in their living room with the lights off listening to
music, very quietly on the gramophone... Was that jazz?
Come in, Master Warweser... Look at you! You've got
your flesh poking out of your shirt like a Haarlem
blacksmith.

MARK: This is a surprise.

JAKOB: Mark.

MARK: How was Wettelbrunn?

JAKOB: We hoped Geli would get it out of my system.

MARK: And?

JAKOB: Can you see the cemetery from here?

MARK: You can always see the cemetery from here.
(*They hug.*)

JAKOB: I'll not wash...

MARK: Neither will I. I love you.

JAKOB: I love you.

JAKOB SNR: Rebekka, pinch me!

REBEKKA: One thing follows another, if you make the
soup, then you'll have to eat it...

JAKOB SNR: Let's eat!

REBEKKA: Sing the Sch'ma!

JAKOB SNR: Pour me some red wine!

*Later. A dark night, thin circle of light from a lantern which MARK
and JAKOB stand under, holding each other, kissing each other goodbye
on the mouth, parting in different directions. SONJA has seen them.
She follows MARK.*

SONJA: Mark! Love!

MARK: Sonja.

SONJA: Here, have a couple of cigarettes!

MARK: You're an angel...

SONJA: Perhaps they're already talking. Saying terrible things. About you and Jakob. Perhaps there's a kangaroo court in the birch trees. On the hill – the ones you were comrades with yesterday – their fathers rolling around in pools of beer at Hiemke's... Krista's mother had to drag her out of the lake by the hair yesterday, she'd gone swimming in her brother's new SS jacket, the mother was shouting how Hitler's finest had beaten her girl's brains out at Colditz Castle.... I keep seeing blood in my dreams. A lot of bright red blood with dark lumps in it running down the window in my dreams.

MARK: Sshhh

SONJA: But the two of you are still having a fine time, here in the Reich? Are you alright in the head, boy?! – They grabbed Hardy clean out of my bed! He had inflamed kidneys. Forty degree fever at night. Do you know how painful that is, lying on inflamed kidneys, how much it hurts?! Then there's banging on the door, after midnight, Gestapo[21]. He thought they were a hallucination, didn't react to any of their orders. So they pulled him out of the room by the legs and down the stairs, the many, many stairs all the way down from seventh heaven... where we were living. His head kept banging on the steps. Bang, bang, bang. I've not had a single card since then from that big new camp... Sometimes they send the wives urns. Horrible – little bones in the ashes!

MARK: Sshh, Sonja! Be quiet!!

SONJA: (*Lamenting, by the end, shouting.*) I should have known which way round you were ages ago, I should have known! And I was the one went and showed him to you at sunrise! Didn't I? I introduced you in the pink morning light! So I end up being the bloody matchmaker!

Scene 8

By Griebnitz Lake

Crooked trunk of a dead birch tree. KRISTA enters carrying a basket with many mushrooms and a large bunch of heather from the wood. Her dress is ripped and her hair is wild.

KRISTA: Cuckoo! – Answer me you stupid cuckoo! – Tell me how much longer I've got to live. (*Listens.*) Big round frightened eyes... Cuckoo! (*Silence.*) Cuckoo! (*Silence.*) Cuckoo! Nothing? (*Sits exhausted against the birch trunk.*) It keeps bleeding and bleeding... (*Feels under her dress.*) Been bleeding ever since... (*Brings her hand back out again.*) Eva sanitary pads. Soaked right through again... (*She looks at the blood on her fingers, then wipes her fingers on her dress.*)

PIMPF: (*Coming.*) Let me go now! I want to go home!

KRISTA: Without any mushrooms?! Without any of these mushrooms?!

PIMPF: Witch! You witch! You slag!

KRISTA: Don't you know your Krista any more...

PIMPF: (*Cries.*) I do, Krista, yes, I do
(*Sound of a motor bike, approaching, hunting, breaks off.*)

KRISTA: Brother's bike.. my brother.. He's still angry with me. Because of his black jacket with the silver mirrors... (*Runs off, dragging PIMPF with her.*)

PETER HUNDT: (*Runs to the birch with his last remaining strength, screams.*) Who are they after?

MARK: (*Falls on the ground, stays there lying on his stomach.*) Me.

MAN WITH SQUINT: Excuse me but if you throw my bike down like that in the heather all the petrol's going to run out...

SS MAN: Shut up! (*Ties PETER HUNDT to the birch tree with a leather belt.*)

MAN WITH SQUINT: Comrade Grohmann...!

SS MAN: After him!

MAN WITH SQUINT: Still wearing your uniform jacket – Jew-lover?! (*Pulls MARK's jacket over his head.*)

SS MAN: Haven't read *Stürmer*[22] for a while – Comrade Jew-lover?! (*Takes one of his boots off.*)

MAN WITH SQUINT: (*Unhooks the rubber truncheon form his belt.*) Criminal elements in Nowawes have recently started believing some Yids are decent human beings.

SS MAN: That's what it says in *Stürmer*!

MAN WITH SQUINT: The Yids are our collective misfortune! (*Taps his truncheon against the strip of bare skin on Mark's back.*) D'you want me to try it? It stings... (*Hits lightly.*)

MARK: (*Screams.*) Peter...!

SS MAN: Shut your mouth! Shut it! (*Pulls Mark's trousers down.*)

PETER HUNDT: Don't be afraid!

MARK: Peter!

SS MAN: (*Hits him with the boot.*) Shut-your-face. So that's what a homo's arse looks like. Right.

MAN WITH SQUINT: Fat cunt!

PETER HUNDT: Don't be afraid...

(*The SS beat MARK on the back and behind with the boot and the truncheon, their frenzy rising with each swing: dull, heavy blows...they pause, MARK doesn't move any more, they find it hard to leave, kick him in the side and then go. MARK moves his hand slowly towards his jacket, awkwardly he manages to cover himself with it.*)

KRISTA: (*Carrying the basket.*) Did it hurt? Well? Did it hurt a lot? Can you stand up? Are you going to stay lying there? Been lying there so long... Flowers on you! Flowers and ribbons.... (*She lets mushrooms and sprigs of heather cascade down over Mark's back.*)

Scene 9

Kitchen Window

Midday the next day at the Warwesers.

VIOLA: Is my boy asleep yet?

WILLO: He's lying on his bed, reading. Did you see those welts?

VIOLA: I wish I wasn't pregnant!

WILLO: Pah – stop that now! Pah – we've all had our problems with Nazi thugs! After 1928, when the Boheme Club moved, we had to walk home through an SA area. And we ran into some fists more than once. Memories.

VIOLA: D'you remember the man who wore women's clothes? Nineteen he was.

WILLO: Lady Heinz.

VIOLA: Lady Heinz sang for us on our sixth wedding anniversary at the Boheme Club.

WILLO: Whatever happened to Lady Heinz? Nothing good I bet...

VIOLA: When he did a striptease you were the only one he gave a feather from his blue boa to!

WILLO: What memories...

(There is a knock at the window, VIOLA opens it, MRS GLÜCKSLEBEN looks in.)

REBEKKA: How many months are you pregnant now?

VIOLA: Seven.

REBEKKA: That's not why I'm here. *(Passes in a casserole dish and a parcel.)*

WILLO: Is that for us?

REBEKKA: Just a pound of coffee. Argentinian. Have you got any coffee in the house?

WILLO: I don't know...

VIOLA: And what's in there?

REBEKKA: A turkey breast. In white sauce. For the boy. I thought I'd best pre-cook it. All you need to do is warm it through. – I'm so sorry.

VIOLA: You don't have to be!

WILLO: There are whispers going round Nowawes. Jakob got...

REBEKKA: Jakob's in Caputh, at his teacher's flat, Miss Selig. Awful pains in his back, his top lip somewhere

between blue and purple – that's what he says on the
phone – two shadowy bullies in big coats, Berlin number
plate, ran straight into his bike, just before he got to
school, it was lucky he wasn't still in the forest! I can't
get over to Miss Selig's today, it's impossible to even
talk to my husband about the horse, no-one's flogging
that horse, he grumbles, he's at the shop putting bars up
on all the windows... Sympathy?! Visiting sick-beds?!
Not me!

WILLO: Would you like me to take you in the car?

REBEKKA: No, no, no! – I want to tie Jakob to a woman
and beat him until he finally does it with her. As if we
didn't have enough problems!

VIOLA: Why don't you come in Rebekka – I'll show you
the baby clothes.

REBEKKA: As if we didn't have enough problems...

WILLO: Now come in and Viola'll show you the baby
clothes... (*Pulls her in through the window.*)

REBEKKA: Is your husband mad? Grabbing me by the
armpits and dragging me through the window?

VIOLA: Your husband's another fine one – with that horse
of his.

REBEKKA: You can say that again. – Will you show me the
clothes for the baby?

WILLO: And I'll make some coffee. Would you like a tot to
go with it, Rebekka? From the 1924 bottle, the same one
I just used to put my son to sleep...painkiller. You look
pale.

REBEKKA: The things that happen... You're shaking,
Rabbi Süss, I said... He knew something from the camp
in Esterwege. From a man he'd winkled out of there,
don't ask me how... this man had talked about the
concentration camp all night, then in the morning he'd
gone into the bathroom and slit his wrists... Dr Ehrlicher
bandaged him up, gave him a morphine injection,
calmed him down, then he told them what one of the
Jews had seen: a gypsy woman had come to Esterwege
heavily pregnant, she'd given birth in the hut, don't ask

me how... and hidden the baby inside the hut so it might
live – then it was discovered. Informers. The German
brute calling himself a camp doctor comes along and
stamps on its little head with his boots, kicks the child to
death.

Scene 10

Evening Phone Call

*The phone rings loudly several times, MARK comes slowly, picks up
the receiver.*

JAKOB: Mark – is that you?

MARK: Hey...

JAKOB: Well...

MARK: That's how they punish naughty children...
A warning, eh?

JAKOB: They ran into me but they didn't run me over. If
they'd got me when I was still in the dark forest they'd
have killed me.

MARK: Poor darling.

JAKOB: Poor darling. Tomorrow I'll be home again. I'll
stay the night with Miss Selig in the room over the
classroom. For supper she's cooking us spinach from the
garden and she's just looking in the nest box for eggs.
Can you hear a chirping noise? It's Miss Selig's canary,
called Herzl, his cage is right by the bed. I'm lying in
her virginal bed, where no man has ever lain, the sheets
rustle, untouched by male hands...we're flirting, let me
stroke you...my finger's stroking the bird's head.

MARK: It's singing with joy – tell it you're already spoken
for.

JAKOB: Can you hear it?

MARK: I can hear your sheets rustling. My bed's getting
cold upstairs, my room is lonely, my room is safe. Why
do you have to be so far away to be so close to me
again? I'm shocked that my bed upstairs is empty when
I've just heard the rustle of you in bed, if only you were
in my bed tonight!

JAKOB: Let's talk about that when we see each other. When

I'm at home – and my back's alright – and you're at home. Don't worry – I want to too. I want to be in bed with you, I really do.

MARK: When?

JAKOB: Soon, very soon. I'm not afraid – I trust you now very much, and you already trust me – without saying so. Here's a kiss for you.

MARK: Here's a kiss back!

JAKOB: See you soon. I'll love you forever.

MARK: I'll love you forever.

(*On tape: the sound of wild geese in flight. An autumn leaf falls gently from above.*)

Scene 11

In the Woodshed

JAKOB is building up logs in a pile.

PETER HUNDT: (*Crumpling up the 'Völkischer Beobachter'*) Munich Agreement[23]: Daladier, Mussolini, Chamberlain and Hitler – the Czechoslovak border given to Germany all wrapped up nice and neat with a bow on top…. The Czechs are the majority. Because of a handful of ethnic Germans, Europe's going to explode again.

JAKOB: Henlein[24] and the Sudenten Germans are puppets!

PETER HUNDT: Appeasement politics: England is a monarchic corpse. France a blue and red corpse. War is hurtling towards us.

JAKOB: And a pogrom on the Jews.

PETER HUNDT: Don't worry!

JAKOB: You're smoking Juno? They're women's cigarettes!

PETER HUNDT: Father's given them by grateful patients.

JAKOB: God I wish I was a gynaecologist! I couldn't save myself from all the women. Next year I'm going to grow a moustache…one of those thin pencil ones…

PETER HUNDT: That's just overgrown nostril hair…you really stink of arrogance sometimes…

JAKOB: I want to go to a Swiss boarding school. Lessons in the morning, sport in the afternoons and in the evening a slide show about Florence...

PETER HUNDT: What about Warweser?

JAKOB: It was nothing. I'm not like that... And my back's better again now... (*Breaks a log across his knee, breaks a second log, hisses with pain, grabs his back and falls to his knees.*)

Scene 12

Dream

MARK: (*Waking from the dream; wide awake, in shock.*) There's a woman dangling from the ceiling with her legs tied apart. A baby falls out of her lap still in its umbilical sac. The skin's damp and shiny. Covered in white slime. Jakob cuts it with heavy silver cutlery and eats the body. Peter and I are standing on top of a glistening pile. We're in SS uniforms, with death's head badges. We're standing tall on top of corpses, rows and rows of them, that's why the pile's so pale and glistening. One of the corpses I recognise – it's Jakob, he's lying at my feet, with his eyes wide open. There's still life in his eyes. His penis is covered by a yellowing cloth whose edges are starting to be overgrown with skin. Peter marches up in cavalry trousers, stands over Jakob, legs apart and looks at me with love in his eyes. 'Shall we carry on, Obersturmbannführer?' he asks, his voice ardent, his eyes smitten. 'Yes, Kommandant,' I reply, 'Because I love you...' The buzzing of an electric hair trimmer on a long black cable. We shave Jakob's head. The clippers are blunt, lumps of skin get stuck between the blades, then the bony skull is exposed, my finger runs gently round the joints of the skull. The cartoon character Pato appears out of the distance. I recognise him from one of Jakob's comics as a black ink drawing with dancing limbs, a humanised spider with eight legs. I close my finger on something, perhaps a spider, a threadlike leg trembles against my wrist. And suddenly there's a star in my hand, a sharp metal star whose edges cut into the flesh clenched around it. It flows warm out of my closed hand – I wake. I'm strongly aroused.

(*Sound of a lorry from outside, getting unbearably loud – it goes once round the roundabout on the Goetheplatz with the engine howling, shouts from the passengers, screams from inside the covered lorry, its lights – white animal eyes – appear, blinding, and then vanish. Finally it's quiet.*)

It's raining on my hand.

Scene 13

Call Me

After midnight, darkness and rain, old cemetery, at Petra von Paschke's grave.

MARK: (*Calling softly.*) Sonja? Sonja? – The window over the shop's dark. Are you sleeping soundly, Jakob Glücksleben? And little Sonja, who I can ask about bodily love... We've exchanged every promise and every kiss. Is there nothing more? To sleep with Jakob stomach to stomach... to stroke him so long that he wants everything and to want everything myself till it screams out of me and I out of him... To lie on the cold earth under a dark sky, to bleed in the snow when winter comes... pink snow? We've never seen each other's naked backs... The skin on his hand is softer than mine, but his fingers grabbed hold of mine so painfully when we kissed. Is there nothing more? How long? Till I'm in a grave like this? It's scary here all alone...Sonja? Is that you? Sonja?

(*The rain murmurs and sighs as if from the grave: MARK retreats from the grave in fear step by step.*)

Peter, is that you?

PETER HUNDT: Not Warweser!

MAN IN OVERCOAT: (*Attacks MARK, pushing his arm round his throat from behind.*) Even if this hurts me more than it hurts you... You won't have been spying out here for nothing, you're coming with me, Nazi!

PETER HUNDT: No, no – this is Warweser! It's only Warweser. He's harmless.

MAN IN OVERCOAT: That's what you say...

PETER HUNDT: I'll swear any oath you like. He's my schoolfriend.

MAN IN OVERCOAT: Nowadays they learn to denounce their fathers, their teachers, their friends...that right, Nazi?!

MARK: Not true.

PETER HUNDT: He's the one who's in love with a Jewish boy...

MAN IN OVERCOAT: Oh, him. (*Lets MARK go.*)

MARK: Your neck's bleeding!

MAN IN OVERCOAT: And my arm's hanging here like it's come away from my body... All I can feel is pain...

MARK: Seriously, Peter – his neck's bleeding really badly!

PETER HUNDT: Warweser got beaten up recently till his skin was hanging off.

MAN IN OVERCOAT: Having your skin cut up isn't much.

PETER HUNDT: Aren't you demanding too much of us, Comrade?!

MAN IN OVERCOAT: There was another raid here tonight in the village... They got a whole truckload of us. One was holding a stab wound in his body closed and the air hissed out of the gaping hole in his side... The one next to me had no teeth left in his mouth... spraying blood like a dream of battle. I managed to jump out of the truck. Sonja was there too! The only woman... We tried to protect her from any more blows with our bodies. But she'd had enough of a kicking already... Sometimes she gets so angry she just can't keep her mouth shut... Now the truck's standing quietly in a garden lane outside Kegelheim, the torture chamber, and let's pray to God that Sonja won't feel anything more! – Take your friend home, Hundt! Before he shits himself!

PART THREE

Scene 1

Krista's Death

30th October, an afternoon by Griebnitz Lake.

JAKOB: Are you swimming, Warweser?

MARK: (*Takes all his clothes off.*) You coming?

JAKOB: I can't swim.

MARK: You can't swim?

JAKOB: I used to...in the swimming baths...yeah. But not in the lake. (*Dips his hand in the water.*)

MARK: Well?

JAKOB: Is it not too cold for you?

MARK: I'm freezing.

JAKOB: My first friend...Karl...at the school in the forest... wasn't like you. He'd stroke me as fast as I could breathe – staring at the door in case anyone came in. It wouldn't have mattered. They were liberal.

MARK: So you're not fresh as the dew?

JAKOB: (*Picks something up off the ground.*)

MARK: I am..

JAKOB: (*Showing his hand.*) I was rescuing a snail.

MARK: It's crawling all over your hand now.

JAKOB: (*Looking at his hand.*) Your body... it's – magnificent, Warweser. I've got a hairier stomach than you. Your arse with all those scars moves me. Let's get married!

MARK: Only you're allowed to see them...

JAKOB: On our wedding night.

MARK: How are we going to do that? Get married...

JAKOB: I'm a Jew – I told the friends I made on holiday about it quite casually. Sometimes I scream it desperately at my face in the mirror -- I'm a Jew! There were plenty of us and it was a beautiful life in that thriving community. I can still see myself sitting at the

long tables we had for religious festivals, indoors and
outdoors, at all the weddings, births and deaths I
attended. If two Jews love each other, they go to the
Rabbi...the Jewish thinkers that are left have become
quite radical. Mr Süss is the leading Jew in the city, Dr
Ehrlicher looks after his district, when everybody calls
you a criminal, you end up thinking as radically as a
gangster. I feel we need a strong hand to guide us, a firm
heart to bless us and a sharp eye to watch over us. I can
make us an appointment to see the Jewish bosses... Shall
we do it?

MARK: Yes – to your mirror image in the black water...

(*Long silence. KRISTA comes creeping on quietly.*)

KRISTA: Are you lovers?

MARK: Don't shout, Krista...

KRISTA: You're naked, Mark, you're naked!

MARK: So I'm naked...did you bring your army with you
again?

KRISTA: No...

JAKOB: You've ruined your dress...

KRISTA: And you're a Yid!

MARK: Her mind's confused.

KRISTA: It's never been clearer. – Watch yourself Jakob:
my father came home drunk last night, the eye teeth
were poking out of his mouth, he giggled in a fatherly
way then banged so hard on the kitchen table the legs
gave way... Here's the date of the next pogrom, he
shouted, all over the Reich, and he tore the last October
page out of the calendar. Nazism still hasn't really taken
hold in Nowawes but now there's going to be another
campaign from the top...and it's going to come right to
your door – Jakob, Josh Hanke who lives upstairs, Mrs
Freisinger in Mozartweg, your little temple whose door's
always being defaced and spat on, that's just kids... In
July I went to Colditz Castle on Düben Heath. I sneaked
off by myself for a walk in the heather, then ten SS men
came along on leave from their duties on that boring
heath, and they saw me, I was in the sunshine, and they

went for me. They took my clothes off and each of them went on me once. And when they'd all finished, they stood in a circle around me – I was lying there on the ground half-dead – and on the command of three they all urinated on me... I can't stand it...and you're going round naked...

MARK: (*Dressing quickly.*) I'm dressed again now... I'm just fastening my belt!

KRISTA: The ghost in my head gets bigger, not smaller. Now I'm being sent to the madhouse in Görden, next door to the prison. There I'll get an injection for not deserving to live, and I was on the side of the Reich, doesn't one of the élite stay one of the élite? I've got my wedding dress on. I'm taking my brother's nice jacket with me, fisherman's leads in the pockets to weigh me down, the boots are little Pimpf's, I knocked him out in the graveyard with this stone here... These tight boots won't let go of my thrashing feet however long I fight death. Farewell.

MARK: Krista!

KRISTA: Let me into the water, don't follow me, let go!

MARK: Watch what you're doing with that stone... Krista!

KRISTA: (*Grapples with the boys, flails about her with the stone, escapes, runs.*) I never loved you!

JAKOB: Go after her! Help her!

MARK: (*Shouting after her.*) Krista! Krista!

Scene 2

Farewell

St. Anthony's church. KRISTA's open coffin, at the head of which the young man with the squint stands to attention. PIMPF crouches beside the coffin, his head hidden in his hands as a song is sung by the congregation from the pews.

MARK: (*Meets PETER, flowers in hand, in a low voice.*) How's school? My sick note runs out on Monday.

PETER HUNDT: Terrible.

MARK: Try to think of the good times we had!

PETER HUNDT: I've seen too much of you in bad times: sweating all over my sheets, bleeding on my shoes, and one night at the cemetery... I wish I hadn't seen you there at all!

MARK: Nothing about Sonja – since...

PETER HUNDT: Sshh!

MARK: I recognised him – that man...

PETER HUNDT: Shut up!

MARK: He was our teacher, when we were juniors, he banned the cane...ages ago...those were times, eh... I used to play rounders in the yard with a Red...

PETER HUNDT: In those days...we still played 'Soviet Russia' in the forest, pretended we were partisans... Jakob used to play with us too...

MARK: I'd forgotten that. What was he?

PETER HUNDT: Your lieutenant...

MARK: Was he? – I suppose that's what we're still playing.

PETER HUNDT: All the way to the gallows.

MARK: No... We stop when it gets dark... when the lights come on, it's time to go home for supper...

PETER HUNDT: Yes... with our severed heads served up neatly on a plate... lost expressions and tongues hanging right out.

MARK: Don't...

PETER HUNDT: Quick, let's say goodbye to Krista, before I decide I want to be walled up in a Catholic church.

MARK: D'you remember what the sermon was like when they took power? Greeted by a forest of arms all reaching up to God... I didn't understand the words but I'll never forget the emotion... I feel frightened now... (*Approaches the coffin boldly, lays down his flowers, hurriedly stretches out his arm, and leaves quickly, almost running. PETER follows him. Outside.*)

MARK: Bye then, see you tomorrow, at school.

PETER HUNDT: Speak today for tomorrow we die... Goodbye. Give Jakob my best wishes, and good luck...

MARK: In that case: Goodbye, I always liked you.

Scene 3

In the Jewish temple.

RABBI SÜSS: Doctor?

DR EHRLICHER: Someone's coming.

RABBI SÜSS Is it the coal at last?

DR EHRLICHER: You've sent the cart the wrong way you're always so disorganised.

RABBI SÜSS: Shouldn't those boys be at school at this time of day?

DR EHRLICHER: You make the appointments then!

RABBI SÜSS: Rebekka's son.

DR EHRLICHER: And his homo...

RABBI SÜSS: Probably reminds you of the case in 1934.

DR EHRLICHER: And you of the one in 1892!

JAKOB: Mother sends her best wishes, everything at home is fine.

DR EHRLICHER: And with you too, Mark Warweser?

MARK: My mother'll be going into labour any day now.

DR EHRLICHER: Then you ought to be at home.

JAKOB: His father's there.

DR EHRLICHER: That's alright then.

MARK: (*Picking up MR SÜSS's crutch.*) You dropped you crutch...here.

RABBI SÜSS: Thank you very much, young man!

DR EHRLICHER: The air here freezes right in front of your face – mother winter's coming.

RABBI SÜSS: In the last winter of the war my boots froze and never came off my feet again.

DR EHRLICHER: Jewish marriages aren't legal.

RABBI SÜSS: If Jewish marriages were legal, we could never dare go ahead with this one...

DR EHRLICHER: You're not a rabbi!

RABBI SÜSS: If the rabbi knew about this he'd come walking back barefoot!

DR EHRLICHER: And spit in your faces!

RABBI SÜSS: Stop you, you youngsters.

DR EHRLICHER: I'm supposed to give you a Jewish wedding, Warweser? This is a joke. I'm not in the mood for jokes.

RABBI SÜSS: Old Mrs Freisinger is in the crate behind my desk. She wants to be sent to the Holy Land. We'll do it.

DR EHRLICHER: Can you smell her yet, lads?

RABBI SÜSS: Look at that snow out there... What can we do – send the dead to Jerusalem, marry two boys who are obviously in love, what else? Tell me what else I can do and I'll do it, immediately!

DR EHRLICHER: Kill Hitler like a dog, silence his propaganda machine, forcibly reeducate the German people, apart from that nothing – Acquire false passports, spy out passages on ships, sweet-talk the Reich's legal system, fail, fail by less. Chemically convert the hot anger in your stomach into cold anger in your head. Hide that cold anger behind constructive help. Your evident sweetness and friendliness, Süss, hides nothing less than cold anger, Süss! You're the caricature of a particularly sweet old fool!

RABBI SÜSS: See the snow outside! A blizzard like in Galicia! There's going to be a wedding in the house, let's do it, we will be committing a punishable offence, we will anger the Lord – there's going to be a wedding in the house! Tomorrow I am not available under any circumstances, the day after we are not available under any circumstances...

DR EHRLICHER: Under certain circumstances we might be available the day after tomorrow! At eight o'clock in the evening, I'll write it down – eight o'clock in the evening – a joke...a little joining together. I need to buy a kessef, have you got three Reichsmarks with you?

JAKOB: My ring size is seven...

DR EHRLICHER: We'll use silver...we'll use iron...you must have fasted that day...

RABBI SÜSS: Are you looking forward to it?

DR EHRLICHER: Remember to fast!

Scene 4

The Marriage. Part 1

9th November 1938, 20.00 hours

At the WARWESERS'.

VIOLA: *(Pacing up and down)* I couldn't keep supper down last night, felt awful.

MARK: *(Pacing up and down in a different direction.)* I felt awful this morning, having breakfast. It's against the rules. Afterwards I went out into the garden and stuck my fingers down the back of my throat.

VIOLA: Today I put my bread out for the cranes, just like the day you were born.

MARK: I didn't have any bread this afternoon!

VIOLA: Even the maternity dress is too small for me now.

MARK: I couldn't get into my black civilian trousers...

VIOLA: Are you pregnant too?

MARK: That's not funny!

VIOLA: Are you wearing your old suit jacket, Mark? Then you should tuck the white shirt into your trousers...
(Tucks MARK's shirttails into his breeches.)

MARK: Your body's heaving.

VIOLA: It's Anna banging on the wall.

MARK: It's not a joke, Mama!

VIOLA: It's hurting my back, just my back – was that a contraction?

MARK: Shall I tell Dr Ehrlicher?

VIOLA: Why? Will you be seeing him?

MARK: Father's outside... He's just knocking the dirt off his shoes on the step... There's father, thank God!
(WILLO appears.)

VIOLA: There's a pain in my back, nothing at the front yet. Was that a contraction?

WILLO: Have they started already? Shall I call Dr Ehrlicher's house?

MARK: You won't find him there tonight.

WILLO: Why not?!

MARK: I've got to go!

WILLO/VIOLA:(*After MARK.*) When are you coming back? Aren't you going to tell us anything?

MARK: I will. Later. (*Runs.*) Wish me luck...

WILLO: Wait, I'll put the outside light on, you'll fall on those icy stairs...

MARK: (*Picking himself up again.*) I just did. (*Exit running.*)

WILLO: Mark?! Damn... Are you alright, Viola?

VIOLA: (*Having a contraction.*) A good home... a good way of life. Plenty of love under one roof.

Scene 5

The Marriage. Part 2

Half past eight to nine o'clock.

In the temple.

MARK: With my eyes closed, I kiss your left cheek, your right cheek...

JAKOB: It was the rotten air of the ultramodern city nearby which drove me into the the arms of a homosexual...

MARK: Are you ashamed of me?

JAKOB: I'm ashamed of me, Warweser!

MARK: And stop calling me 'Warweser'!

JAKOB: With my eyes closed, I kiss your left cheek, your right cheek...

(*SÜSS and EHRLICHER arrive. SÜSS sits down behind his desk, pours wine into a glass, EHRLICHER leads MARK and JAKOB forward by the elbow. SÜSS puts up a large black umbrella, which he holds over MARK and JAKOB during the ceremony.*)

RABBI SÜSS: (*As Baal Kidduschin.*)

Then I saw a new heaven and a new earth; for the first heaven and the first earth had passed away, and the sea was no more. (*Passes MARK and JAKOB the glass, each takes a sip from the same glass.*) Then I saw an angel coming

down from heaven, holding in his hand the key to the
bottomless pit and a great chain.

(*DR EHRLICHER: passes MARK the kessef, the ring he
bought and MARK puts the ring on JAKOB's finger.*)

Then I saw a great white throne and the one who sat on
it; the earth and the heaven fled from his presence, and
no place was found for them.

DR EHRLICHER: Now comes the Jihud, the withdrawal.

(*SÜSS and EHRLICHER leave the room.*)

MARK: Are we going to have dinner together when we've
finished here?

JAKOB: Yes of course! At the Eden. They still let Jews in
there. The taxi's probably already here.

MARK: I've not got any money...

JAKOB: You're not paying. Rabbi Süss is paying.

(*SÜSS and EHRLICHER return and resume their places.*)

RABBI SÜSS: And the beast was captured and with it the
false prophet who had performed in its presence the
signs by which he deceived those who had received the
mark of the beast and those who worshipped its image.
These two were thrown alive into the lake of fire that
burns with sulfur. (*Passes the wine to MARK and JAKOB for
them each to sip from the same glass.*) And the rest were
killed by the sword of the rider on the horse, and all the
birds were gorged with their flesh.

(*DR EHRLICHER places the glass on the floor.*)

DR EHRLICHER: At the end of the ceremony the wine
glass is placed at the bridegroom's feet and he treads on
it with his foot.

(*MARK treads on the glass.*)

RABBI SÜSS: Just as this glass may never again be whole,
so may this union never be dissolved... Thank you for
your attention.

DR EHRLICHER: Quick, quick! To the Eden! The taxi's
been waiting for ages...

MARK: We were a merry group sitting in the Eden. One
night in November 1938. We ate snails in a dish of white
salt with special snail forks, and there was a great deal of

laughter. Mr. Süss's crutch glided along the red carpet, he went to the telephone, when he returned he was no longer the same. Loudspeaker cars crept along the Tauentzien screaming: 'Herschel Grynzspan[25] you Jewish cunt' . For dessert we had the deliciously wicked 'Fall of Babylon'. And sang Prince Pückler's praises. We all breathed the Eden's perfumed air and Jakob fell half asleep on my shoulder. Four glasses of cognac – Dr Ehrlicher's treat – cheers. It's the pogrom. A hurried departure. Holding our arms up to cover our faces as we scrambled into the taxi. And drove at speed out of the crashing city – all along the Tauentzien and the Kurfürstendamm, both sides of the street had SS men with civilian jackets over their uniforms, smashing windows with iron bars, carrying lists of Jewish houses... Quick, quick, back to the quiet of home!

Scene 6

Reichskristallnicht[26]. Part 1

Living room of the WARWESERS' house.

DR EHRLICHER: (*Arrives with MARK and JAKOB.*) The Warwesers' house – lights on in all the windows. Are they having a party? Dancing in every room...

MARK: Damn...

DR EHRLICHER: Damn, damn...

(*They enter.*)

WILLO: (*Shouting.*) It's gone eleven o'clock... What were you thinking of, eh? What were you thinking of?

DR EHRLICHER: Go to bed, Mr. Warweser! It's all over. The boys are here, and unharmed. Lights out! And don't panic... I've got to fetch Süss, the taxi's waiting just outside the village... (*About to leave.*)

REBEKKA: (*Hastily, screaming.*) Thank God, Dr Ehrlicher!

JAKOB: You – here...?

REBEKKA: Are you married?

JAKOB: Yes...

WILLO: (*Shouts.*) What's all this supposed to mean?! I could give you a right...!

121

DR EHRLICHER: (*Shouts back.*) Quiet! Quiet, turn the lights out and calm down will you! – Right.

REBEKKA: His wife's having the baby.

DR EHRLICHER: (*Shouts.*) And all you do is sit around here?!

WILLO: (*Shouts.*) We couldn't get hold of you!

DR EHRLICHER: (*Shouts.*) There is the city clinic and the respected Mr... Dr Hundt!

VIOLA: Not Dr Hundt!

REBEKKA: (*Holding VIOLA back.*) No love, no...not Dr Hundt...

DR EHRLICHER: Mrs Warweser...

WILLO: I tried getting my car, to take Viola to the clinic... D'you think I'm daft?! – I go out there, the night smells of tar and I hear a drumming... like wooden spoons on washbasins, and all the Jews are sneaking out of their back yards... Mr, Warweser, your car's on fire! – and I can hear the drumming... smell the burning...

DR EHRLICHER: Mrs Warweser!

VIOLA: It feels like a hedgehog thrashing round inside me... Waves of tension that drain me...

DR EHRLICHER: Have you timed them?

REBEKKA: Four minutes...

DR EHRLICHER: You've picked a fine time for it, girl – Mrs Warweser – how big is your kitchen table? Come on, Rebekka! (*The three exit.*)

JAKOB SNR: Can I offer my congratulations?

WILLO: Not to me, not yet.

JAKOB SNR: Our two sons.

WILLO: There's schnapps there.

JAKOB SNR: These lights will attract attention. A candle's enough.

WILLO: Very well...

JAKOB SNR: To life.

WILLO: Couldn't he have told his father? His father, his jolly and faithful friend... Who'd still got a blue feather boa...

DR EHRLICHER: (*From the kitchen.*) Viola... Viola, you've

got to let me see, or else it's still going to hurt in January! Alright, alright – the table's not strong enough... (*Shouts.*) Mr Warweser, Glücksleben, come here!

(*WILLO and JAKOB SNR follow the shouts; MARK and JAKOB, looking at each other quickly in agreement, leave by the other side of the room.*)

Scene 7

Reichskristallnicht. Part 2

In the WARWESERS' house, upstairs in MARK's room.

They fold down the bed. Nothing is said while JAKOB slips his clothes off. He walks over to MARK, leans back against his friend, pulls MARK's arms over his shoulders and places MARK's hands over his genitals.

MARK: Hey... I've still got my clothes on... let me take them off... (*Removes himself from JAKOB, pulls the curtain across in front of the washstand and disappears behind it, pulls the curtain open and is wearing a red silk dressing gown and red leather slippers on his feet.*)

JAKOB: Is that Warweser? I'm grinning.

MARK: Can't you ever stop calling me by my surname? Go on then, grin! This is your Warweser.

JAKOB: That's my Warweser. I'll have to get used to it. Like the fiery glow from outside.. or is it the red of your silk, King David?

MARK: This is me. Insignificant. Homosexual. Defenceless. Homosexual. What are you grinning at?

JAKOB: Your bony feet in those Turkish slippers! – Are you cross with me?

MARK: Yeah, a bit.

JAKOB: Is that why you won't love me?

MARK: Yes...

(*Silence.*)

JAKOB: (*Shouts.*) Warweser?!

MARK: (*On the verge of tears, repressing a shout.*) Fucking wedding night!

JAKOB: I didn't have to, Warweser! I could have had anyone, anyone... I'm good stock, you're bad... All cosy and neat in a poky little room with a rampaging mob behind the flowery shutters... If this was Weimar, I'd never have looked at you, never have loved you... I'd have been flamboyant and heartless. Today I'm quiet... it's so homely here... (*Walks up to MARK.*) You're slightly taller...

MARK: (*Takes his slippers off.*) We're the same height...

JAKOB: How did you get here? The path over the crags is dangerous. Those rocks are sharp...

MARK: What?!

JAKOB: I'm leaving tomorrow.

MARK: Oh, on holiday...

JAKOB: No, for my grave... Griebnitz Lake.

MARK: (*Throws his red coat on the floor.*) Jakob, stop mucking about! (*Kneels by the bed.*)

DR EHRLICHER: Now help me, or else it'll still hurt in January...

(*VIOLA's harsh scream; downstairs heavy knocking at the front door.*)

PIMPF: Can I say it -

MAN WITH SQUINT: In the name of the Führer -

PIMPF: Open up! Gestapo!

The End.

Translator's Notes

1 – p. 66, HITLER, Adolf Hitler (1889-1945) became *Führer* (absolute leader) of the National Socialist German Workers' Party, otherwise known as the Nazis, in 1921. A constitutional crisis led to him being appointed Chancellor of Germany in January 1933 although the Nazis had a minority of seats in the Reichstag (parliament) and a minority of the popular vote. Within a year, the Reichstag had been burnt to the ground in mysterious circumstances, elections suspended, other political parties banned and the Nazi party indissolubly joined to the state. This totalitarian regime, the Third Reich, was to persist until Germany's military defeat in World War II.

2 – p. 67, THE YOUTH, The Hitler Youth (*Hitlerjugend* or *HJ*) was a youth organisation started by the National Socialist party to prepare young people for party membership and service in the armed forces. Membership was compulsory from the ages of 10-18.

3 – p. 69, THE GERMAN LEAGUE, The German Girls' League (*Bund Deutscher Mädchen* or *BDM*) was a subsidiary organisation within the Hitler Youth movement for girls. Membership was compulsory for 10-17 year olds.

4 – p. 69, ROSENBERG, Alfred Rosenberg (1893-1946), chief Nazi ideologist and author of *The Myth of the Twentieth Century*.

5 – p. 69, STREICHER, Julius Streicher (1885-1946), Nazi ideologist and founder editor of *Stürmer*. Gauleiter of Franconia.

6 – p. 69, SA, (full name: *Stürmabteilung*) Storm troopers or brownshirts. A division of the Nazi party, begun very early in its history, used to guard the Nazi's own meetings and intimidate enemies.

7 – p. 73, EMMI SONNEMANN, Actress, married to Hermann Goering, Commander of Hitler's Air Force.

8 – p. 74, SCHICKLGRÜBER, Original surname of Adolf Hitler's (illegitimate) father.

9 – p. 78, UFA, Founded in 1917 as Universum Film, the main German film studios, located close to the scenes of the play in Babelsberg.

10 – p. 80, SCHLAGETER MEMORIAL, Albert Schlageter (1894-1923) was a Nazi party member executed for organising resistance to French and Belgian military occupation of the Ruhr.

11 – p. 82, HORST WESSEL SONG, Famous Nazi marching song in memory of Horst Wessel, a young Nazi party member killed in a fight in Berlin in 1930, who was glorified as a martyr to the Nazi cause.

12 – p. 83, MAGNUS HIRSCHFELD, (1868-1935) Pioneering sexologist, director of the first Insititute of Sexology and co-founder of the World League for Sexual Reform. His institute was closed in 1933 and his books publicly burnt. He died in exile.

13 – p. 86, BALDUR BOYS, Baldur von Schirach (1907-1974) was Reich Youth Leader in overall charge of the Hitler Youth and German Girls' League.

14 – p. 91, NUREMBERG LAWS, Two laws passed at the Nazi party congress in Nuremberg in 1935 outlawing marriage and extra-marital sexual contact between Jews and 'those of German blood' and introducing two-tier citizenship, distinguishing between Aryan 'citizens of the Reich' and Jewish 'citizens of the state.'

15 – p. 93, MAX SCHMELING, (born 1905) German boxer, world heavyweight champion 1930-32.

16 – p. 95, SS, (Full name *Schutzstaffel*; defence detachment) Blackshirts. An élite military organisation which began as Hitler's personal guard and later ran the Concentration Camps.

17 – p. 95, *THE SORROWS OF YOUNG WERTHER,* Classic novel by J. W. von Goethe with a distinctly gloomy reputation.

18 – p. 98, THAT RÖKK WOMAN, Marika Rökk (born 1913) Cabaret performer and film actress in numerous UFA features of the time. A former child star.

19 – p. 98 GERTRUD KOLMAR, (1894-1943) German poet. Jewish.

20 – p. 99, THÄLMANN, Ernst Thälmann (1886-1944) Leader of the German Communist Party from 1925. Arrested by the Nazis in 1933. Later died in Buchenwald Concentration Camp.

21 – p. 102, GESTAPO, (full title: *Geheime Staatspolizei*) Secret police. Independent, ruthless and loyal to Hitler. Cultivated the use of informers.

22 – p. 104, *STÜRMER,* Nazi newspaper founded in 1923, notorious for its anti-semitism.

23 – p. 108, MUNICH AGREEMENT, An agreement made at the Munich Conference on 29th September 1938 between Adolf Hitler, Eduard Daladier (France), Neville Chamberlain (England), and Mussolini (Italy) annexing the Sudetenland, hitherto part of Czechoslovakia, to Germany.

24 – p. 108, HENLEIN, Konrad Henlein (1898-1945) Leader of the pro-Nazi Sudeten Party and subsequently Governor of the Sudetenland.

25 – p. 121, HERSCHEL GRYNZSPAN, (born 1921-??) Jew who assassinated diplomat Ernst von Rath in the German

embassy in Paris on 7th November 1938 in protest at his parent's deportation from Germany to Poland. Arrested by the French authorities, he is presumed to have died in prison.

26 – p. 121, REICHSKRISTALLNACHT, A night of hitherto unprecedented violence against Jewish homes and businesses on 9th-10th November 1938 sanctioned by the Nazi leadership and organised by the SA and SS.

Printed in the USA
CPSIA information can be obtained
at www.ICGtesting.com
LVHW020843171024
794056LV00002B/377